Puffin Books
Editor: Kaye Webb

THE CRUI[illegible]

'Pencil and paper ple[illegible]garty. 'I want you to relate to me all th[illegible] that would make your brothers green with e[illegible]y, and I will write them down.'

'A sea voyage!' said Sophie.

'Desert islands!' said Emma.

'Pirates!' said Rose.

'Sharks!' said Lucy.

'Savages!' said Emma.

'Buried treasure!' said Sophie.

'Typhoons!' said Emma (and 'Shipwrecks!' and 'Cannibals!' and 'Diamonds!' too).

Suddenly it looked as if all these adventures were really going to happen, for at the top of the list Aunt Hegarty had written *Itinerary for Voyage by Ship with Nieces.*

And come true they did, starting almost immediately when their mysterious and long-lost cousin Annie turned up from the orphanage, and it was as well she did because it was Annie who would have such an influence on their fates when they met the pirates and cannibals . . .

Ursula Moray Williams is already well known and loved for her books in the Puffin series, *Adventures of the Little Wooden Horse*, *Gobbolino the Witch's Cat* and *Johnnie Tigerskin*. This funny and satisfying story will make her an even firmer favourite.

For girls of eight and over.

Ursula Moray Williams

The Cruise of the 'Happy-Go-Gay'

Illustrated by Gunvor Edwards

Penguin Books

Penguin Books Ltd, Harmondsworth,
Middlesex, England
Penguin Books Australia Ltd, Ringwood,
Victoria, Australia

First published by Hamish Hamilton 1967
Published in Puffin Books 1971

Made and printed in Great Britain by
Cox & Wyman Ltd,
London, Reading and Fakenham
Set in Intertype Plantin

To E. Freda Williams

Contents

Chapter One

The Nieces

'At six o'clock I have to see a man about a boat,' said Aunt Hegarty to her five nieces, putting on her Admiral's hat. 'You can come with me if you like. Just pile the tea-things in the sink for Bella.'

The nieces had come to stay with Aunt Hegarty because they were bored at home.

Their brothers, they said, had all the fun.

They rowed, they shot, they played cricket, they played truant, they had dogs and dogwhips, catapults and caterpillars. They shouted and sang and sometimes swore, they ate everything that was put on the table and nearly everything that was put in the larder. They lost their tempers and nearly all the tennis balls and took up so much space that there seemed little left for their sisters to breathe in and absolutely nothing for them to do but be little ladies, like the precious daughters of their gracious sovereign Victoria. God save the Queen.

'It is a tragedy for nieces to be bored,' Aunt Hegarty wrote to their parents. 'It is your fault of course. Send them to stay with me, bringing warm underclothes designed for danger. Do not send their brothers with them. I detest boys.'

The Mamma and Papa of the five nieces replied by telegram:

'Will send girls on railway tomorrow. Please define danger. How much and how dangerous.'

Aunt Hegarty replied, also by telegraph:

'To be bored is much more dangerous. Will meet train tea-time.'

In reply to which came one further telegraph:

'Urge you take brothers too. Reply paid.'

Aunt Hegarty replied: 'No.'

So when she met the train there were only Sophie, Lucy, Rose, Harriet and Emma, carrying little bags. Aunt Hegarty's man-of-all-work called Mr Mumpus pushed their bigger trunks home on a handcart. Aunt Hegarty walked with her nieces, now and then catching a butterfly in the collapsible net she carried attached to her belt.

Her house when they reached it was an old coastguard's cottage, near the sea. No wonder there had been no pony cart to meet them, for the property was so small it had no stable – only a low, whitewashed wall surrounding a very little terrace, paved with cobblestones, and a small painted front door, sunk so deeply into the wall that it looked as if someone had pushed a cork in too far.

Over the door hung a ship's lantern, illuminating Aunt Hegarty's coat-of-arms (a sea serpent coiled round an anchor) and under the coat-of-arms was her motto: 'I Come Back Alive!'

Aunt Hegarty, as the nieces knew, was an intrepid explorer, in the days when other ladies stayed at home and painted lamp-shades. Inside the cottage the sitting-room and the parlour were decorated with treasures Aunt Hegarty had collected in her travels, elephants' feet, buffaloes' horns, cowboys' lariats, matadors' capes, rajahs' boots, cobras' hoods, Eskimos' hats and many strange moths and insects arranged in a life-like fashion on twigs inside glass cases.

While they were studying these Aunt Hegarty's maid Bella put muffins on the table and Mumpus, the man-of-all-work, clattered up the stairs for a fifth time carrying the last of the trunks.

'You seem to have brought a great deal of luggage between you,' said Aunt Hegarty. 'Woollen drawers, flannel petticoats and warm cloaks would have been adequate for our travels. And your velvets for Sundays. You will not need gloves, and sunbonnets are better than hats for the tropics.'

The five nieces were agog to hear where they were going and what was expected of them, but it was not until they had all finished eating that Aunt Hegarty pushed aside the muffin dish and said:

'Now quickly! Pencil and paper please! I want you to relate to me all the adventures that would make your brothers green with envy, and I will write them down.'

'A sea voyage!' said Sophie.

'Desert islands!' said Emma.

'Pirates!' said Rose.

'Sharks!' said Lucy.

'Savages!' said Emma.

'Buried treasure!' said Sophie.

'Underground tunnels!' said Harriet.

'Typhoons!' said Emma.

'Shipwrecks!' said Emma.

'Cannibals!' said Emma.

'Diamonds!' said Emma.

'Oh shut up, Emma!' said the others.

Aunt Hegarty wrote fast.

'Anything else?' she asked.

'Everything else!' said Emma. 'Lagoons and sea-serpents and mermaids and palm trees and stars like Japanese lanterns and moonlight on the sea.'

'Boys don't envy us things like that!' the others scoffed.

'I love them,' said Emma.

'Good,' said Aunt Hegarty, 'I think we have a comprehensive list here. I am going to pin it up on the door. Then anyone who wishes can scratch off any item she pleases, before six o'clock. At six o'clock I am going to see a man about a boat.'

The nieces clustered round the piece of paper.

They saw that Aunt Hegarty had written on top of the list:

'*Itinerary for Voyage by Ship with Nieces.*'

And suddenly small shivers began to rush down their spines. They did not dare to cross out many of the items for fear Aunt Hegarty should think them cowards and send them home, but all her sisters crossed out Emma's.

Emma took it very calmly. She just waited till the others were piling the tea-things in the sink and then she wrote them all down again.

Chapter Two

Buying a Boat

The five nieces followed Aunt Hegarty down to the harbour, where a man was holding a little rowing boat on a piece of rope, like a dog. The little boat was bobbing about on the water, playing a kind of hide-and-seek with the orange peel and newspaper that chased each other round its bows. It was a newly varnished boat with the name *Lady Gay* painted in black letters on its prow, and the nieces fell in love with it immediately.

'Where are the oars?' Aunt Hegarty demanded.

The man produced a pair of oars, one blue and one red.

'Two oars are quite useless,' said Aunt Hegarty. 'There are six of us and we shall need at least one each, probably two. I shall not buy your boat.'

The nieces were terribly disappointed. They could hardly bear to turn their backs on the dear little *Lady Gay*, but Aunt Hegarty was flying down the quay and they hurried after her, looking cross.

'It is no use sulking!' Aunt Hegarty shouted over her shoulder. 'Where was the cabin? Where was the cook's galley? Where were the bunks? Whoever thought of going to sea without any bunks?'

The nieces were ashamed of their own improvidence. No shelter from the sun, no comfort from the storm, nowhere to lay their heads at night. Of course Aunt Hegarty was right.

She had now checked her flight to survey a large schooner tied up beside the quay and approached by a narrow gangplank, up which she scrambled like a raiding cat, followed by her panting nieces, who broke loose all over the decks like a herd of visiting monkeys.

They swarmed up the companion ways, they clambered on the bridge, they turned the cook's galley inside out and explored the hold and the sleeping quarters.

This time there were so many bunks that a niece sailing in the schooner might sleep in a different bed each night of the voyage, but when she put her hands on the wheel and looked ahead for an imaginary star to steer a course by, no niece could believe that she would ever want to sleep at all.

For above their heads the great sails were furled aloft on masts standing like fingers pointing to the sky, asking silence for a spate of ocean tales and stories. The name upon her prow was the *Golden Harry*.

Aunt Hegarty said she thought it might do.

The nieces almost fainted with joy when she said this, but they nearly fainted again with frustration when Aunt Hegarty added: 'But I shan't make up my mind till I've seen the little steamer down at the end of the dock.' And once more they all scampered after her though there was nothing to be seen at the end of the dock except a dirty-looking smokestack sticking out from behind a shed.

'That is the boat I mean!' said Aunt Hegarty.

The five nieces stopped dead in their tracks. It really did not seem worth going any farther for an object like that.

'Come along!' Aunt Hegarty commanded, so, reluctantly, they came, trailing across the stout gangway on to the narrow deck with no attempt to hide the scornful clatter of their little patent leather boots.

The steamer was small and stout, but shabby, and rusty where it ought to have beeen clean. For many years it had worked as a ferry boat between Piggy Island and Llwllwllchwllyn in Wales but recently Llwllwllchwllyn had built a bridge.

The deck was surrounded by strong white railings and had

seats at intervals, every one of which the nieces tried. Between two of the seats, against the railings, hung a lifebelt, and on the lifebelt was painted the name of the ship: *Happy-Go-Gay*.

It was all very compact and convenient.

The cook's galley was so close to the wheelhouse that the cook had only to stretch out a hand to serve a cup of tea to the steersman standing at the wheel. Below, there were six bunks covered with red and white checked blankets. The pillows rustled when the nieces punched them, and smelt of hay. There was a store-room full of cupboards, and a Captain's cabin and a lounge, lined with seats, in case it rained on deck.

Underneath the lounge was the engine-room full of pistons, levers, cranks, boilers, valves and pressure gauges.

Lucy, who had never dreamed of such a place in the whole of her life, stood open-mouthed, staring at the rods and knobs and other mysteries, longing above all things to bring them to life. She reached out a finger and stroked the pistons. A long streak of oil appeared on the palm of her hand. Lucy looked at it lovingly.

'Well, what do you think of it?' Aunt Hegarty asked on deck. 'Everything here, after all, and sound. Built to last, even if it hasn't.'

'It's horrid!' said Sophie, Harriet and Rose.

'It has a lovely name!' said Emma.

'It's so dull!' said Sophie.

'And dirty!' said Harriet.

'And cheap-looking!' said Rose.

'It's a *dear* boat!' said Emma.

'It has no lovely sails like the *Golden Harry*!' pouted Harriet.

At that moment Lucy's face, streaked with black, appeared at the hatchway.

'It has a *body*!' she said. 'And when the engine goes, its heart beats. I want to live down there all the time and look after the beautiful engines. May I, Aunt Hegarty?'

'We seem to have three for the *Harry* and two for the *Happy-Go-Gay*!' said Aunt Hegarty. Emma and Lucy felt they had already lost and their faces grew sad.

'Which do *you* like best, Aunt Hegarty?' asked Sophie, Harriet and Rose, quite confident of her reply.

'Let us all think again for a moment,' said Aunt Hegarty, sitting down in the Captain's cabin. 'Remember, the weather will not always be fine . . .'

The nieces thought of the rows of bunks and the hide-and-seek they could play below deck in the *Golden Harry*.

'The wind will blow . . .' said Aunt Hegarty, and Harriet

pictured the great sails filling, billowing and swelling, carrying them along towards the seven seas.

'Someone will have to climb up and unfurl the sails,' said Aunt Hegarty. 'And when a storm comes they will have to climb up and take them down again.'

The nieces were silent for a long time.

'I would,' said Emma, 'if I didn't like the *Happy-Go-Gay* better.'

'The decks,' said Aunt Hegarty, 'are very vast and spacious . . .'

(Hopscotch, skipping ropes, Highland dances!)

'And they will have to be scrubbed every day,' she added.

'I like scrubbing,' said Lucy, 'only I would rather clean the *Gay*'s engines.'

'And the hold, I am bound to tell you,' said Aunt Hegarty, 'has rats in it.'

None of the nieces liked rats.

'We will all tie knots in our handkerchiefs,' said Aunt Hegarty. 'One knot for the *Golden Harry* and two for the *Happy-Go-Gay*. Put your handkerchiefs on the table.'

When they examined the handkerchiefs they found Sophie and Harriet had voted for the *Golden Harry* and so had Emma. She wanted to be kind to the others and she quite liked the thought of trimming those great white sails.

Rose had voted for the *Happy-Go-Gay* because of the rats. So of course had Lucy. And so had Aunt Hegarty.

'What do we do now?' said the nieces, perplexed.

'We draw straws,' said Aunt Hegarty promptly.

After some searching two straws were found in the *Happy-Go-Gay*'s hold, which had no rats in it. One straw was longer than the other.

'The long one is the *Golden Harry* and the short one the *Happy-Go-Gay*!' said Aunt Hegarty. 'I shall drop them over the starboard side and whichever reaches the dockside first is the boat we shall buy.'

The nieces crowded to the rail as Aunt Hegarty tossed the straws into the rising tide. A few yards away the water went slap-slap against the wet black walls of the dock, and along the sides of the boat the straws wended their way, at first side by side, then taking independent passages between the scum and the seaweed sharing the water with her keel. At one time the *Golden Harry*'s straw became entangled with a morsel of

floating rope, then it freed itself, while the *Happy-Go-Gay's* straw was forced to sail around a bobbing wooden crate that held it back for several minutes. Then both floated into free water and, several feet apart, they jerked and bobbed and tit-tuped towards the dock.

Aunt Hegarty did not join in the shrieks and exclamations of her nieces. She stood calmly beside the rail, tapping it with her foot, yet Emma sensed her partiality, and they shared the suspense when the *Golden Harry*'s straw began to creep ahead.

'Can you *afford* to buy the schooner if it wins?' she whispered under Aunt Hegarty's elbow.

Aunt Hegarty nodded. 'I shall sell my butterfly collection,' she explained.

But the schooner did not win. By one of the freaks of time and tide it began to lose ground, fell back, swung around, was swept into the side of the ferry boat where it disappeared, while the *Happy-Go-Gay*'s straw, without altering its pace, plodded steadily towards the wall and arrived triumphant.

Emma clasped her hands.

'Good!' said Lucy and Rose.

'It doesn't matter!' said Sophie and Harriet.

'Let's go and choose our bunks!' said Emma.

Chapter Three

Shopping for the Voyage

The next morning was spent in buying stores and fitting out the steamer for the voyage.

The *Happy-Go-Gay* now belonged to Aunt Hegarty and she had not had to sell her butterfly collection.

She gave a long list of groceries to Sophie and ten shillings to Harriet to buy presents for the natives.

Rose took a net bag to the market for vegetables and fruit, to carry them on for a while, and Lucy was sent down to the railway station to have a lesson in stoking boilers.

'What shall I get?' asked Emma.

'I will give you five shillings to spend on indispensables,' said Aunt Hegarty. 'You can use your common sense and please don't waste it.'

Emma went straight to the dictionary and looked up indispensables. It meant things one would not like to be without when travelling across the sea in a ferry steamer.

Sweets, thought Emma, but Aunt Hegarty had already put two pounds of bulls' eyes on the grocery list.

A compass she thought was a good idea, but remembered there was an excellent boxed compass beside the wheel of the *Happy-Go-Gay*.

A calendar! thought Emma, but the year was half over and nobody had any calendars left to sell.

'Here, dearie, you can have the rest of this one for luck!' said a kind stationer's wife who was sorry for her. The calendar had a picture of Highland cattle on it and the months were printed large and clear.

All of a sudden Emma thought of something that might well be called Indispensable. If they had a ship's cat the hold of the *Happy-Go-Gay* would never become infested by rats like the hold of the *Golden Harry*. A cat too was such company and it would be nice to have an animal on board when they set sail. She hurried to find a pet shop.

She had not far to go, but when she arrived it was to find a whole basket of kittens in the window labelled 'To be given away'. Nobody seemed to want her five shillings and Emma was a little vexed, feeling in a strange way, cheated. She took a long time choosing which kitten to have. When she had selected a tabby: 'Is this one clean?' she asked the shopkeeper.

'Bless you dearie, that one was born clean!' said the shopkeeper, picking up the kitten by the scruff of the neck. 'Take two love, and save my drowning of 'em.'

Emma was horrified. 'But could I have *two* for nothing?' she pleaded, thinking, two kittens would keep one another company in the hold.

'Have the lot for nothing!' said the man cheerfully. Before Emma could stop him he had tipped the basketful into a sack and thrust it at her. 'If you don't want 'em, drop 'em in the dock!' he said cheerfully, leaving Emma standing with her mouth open and the bag of kittens dangling from her hand.

Not having the heart to abandon the kittens to the cruel shopman, she was about to leave the shop when a strange sound caught her ear. Somewhere behind the hutches and the wicker baskets and the birdcages, a goat was bleating, and sure enough, tied to the counter and lying on a bed of dirty straw, was a thin black nanny goat.

Emma's heart lightened. Kittens drank milk, nanny goats provided it. And an indispensable need on a voyage was fresh milk. 'How much is the goat please?' she asked.

'Five bob to you miss!' said the shopman promptly.

All her money gone at a blow, but Emma had no qualms. She left the shop with the bag of kittens in one hand and the goat's lead in the other.

Everyone agreed that Emma had shown good sense in buying the goat. She basked in general approval. 'And what's in the bag?' asked her sisters.

'Ship's cats,' said Emma.

She emptied the kittens on to the floor. There were twenty-five of them.

'I will go to sea with *one cat only*,' said Aunt Hegarty.

'Oh, Aunt Hegarty, can't we have one each?' begged the nieces.

'What shall I *do* with them?' wailed Emma, bursting into tears.

'I can think of only one way to get rid of them,' Aunt Hegarty said, while the nieces trembled for the kittens' fate.

'Take all of them except one to the deck of the *Golden Harry* and let them free in the hold.'

Thankfully the nieces collected the kittens and put them back in the bag. They scampered down to the quay, along the gangway and on to the deck of the *Golden Harry*. Emma rescued the kitten of her choice just in time before they emptied

the rest into the hold, shutting their eyes and ears against the dreadful scuttling of rats within. For a moment the scuttling redoubled, with added squeaks and groans, then it died down, as through a crack beneath the hatchway appeared kitten after kitten carrying dead rats and growling like baby tigers. Eyeing the nieces with fury and distrust they trotted away with their trophies to eat them secretly in chosen places.

Emma's kitten mewed frantically to join them, but she clasped it tightly, hoping to woo its small affections with goat's milk.

At home Sophie was checking her list with Aunt Hegarty.

Everything seemed to be there except the bulls' eyes, which the grocer was sending up when they came in.

Rose was in trouble. She had economized on cheap fruit and some of it was bad.

'Oranges may seem dear at twelve a shilling but scurvy may cost your life,' said Aunt Hegarty. Rose went flying back to the shop to exchange the oranges.

Harriet had been to the Penny Bazaar with the natives in mind. She bought a large number of bangles, paper doyleys, matchbox covers painted with the colours of local regiments, glass balls, dutch dolls, tape measures and several brooches with *Mother* in letters made of twisted gold wire. Her ten shillings had given out and she had spent threepence of her own money.

'Thank you, my dear!' said Aunt Hegarty.

At that moment Lucy appeared, perfectly black, and had to be shown everything.

'When Rose comes back we shall have tea,' said Aunt Hegarty.

But hardly was the muffin dish set on the table when there came a ring at the door bell, and Bella poked her head into the drawing-room to say uncertainly:

'Please 'm – there's another niece!'

Chapter Four

The New Niece

'Another *niece*?' said Aunt Hegarty, startled.

'Please 'm, that's what the young lady says!'

The parlour was full of stores and provisions.

'Bring her in here!' said Aunt Hegarty.

When Bella returned she was pushing in front of her a very thin very delicate-looking child with large black eyes and an obstinate expression.

'Brother Charlie's child!' exclaimed Aunt Hegarty in astonishment. The five nieces stared. They had never even heard of brother Charlie. Their own mother, who was Aunt Hegarty's sister, was called Gertrude.

'But brother Charlie is dead!' murmured Aunt Hegarty when the new niece said nothing. 'And sister-in-law Minnie took the children away. She never answered my letters. Is my sister-in-law Minnie still alive, my child?'

The new niece shook her head.

'Then where do you come from?' asked Aunt Hegarty. 'And what is your name, my dear?'

'I live in an orphanage,' said the new niece, 'and my name is Annie.'

'Then how in the world did you hear about us?' Aunt Hegarty said, waving her hand towards the five nieces and the provisions which could be seen bursting out of the parlour door.

'The orphanage porter has an evening paper,' said Annie. 'Last night when I went to fetch fish and chips I read it, on the back . . .'

She pulled a torn fragment of greasy newspaper from the pocket of her grey cloak and handed it to Aunt Hegarty who read aloud:

'LADY EXPLORER BUYS BOAT TO TAKE NIECES ON VOYAGE OF DISCOVERY
The well known traveller and explorer, Miss Hegarty, of Sunset Cottage, St Pilgrim's Bay, is reputed to have bought the old ferry steamer *Happy-Go-Gay*, and is manning it with her nieces for a voyage to the South Seas, a striking example of the new pioneering spirit prevalent among women of today. This is to be strictly an all-women cruise. We are proud of our British maidens and their intrepid leader and wish them *bon voyage* and a safe return to their native shores.'

Aunt Hegarty stared at Annie, who dropped her eyes and twisted her fingers together.

'So you want to come too?' she said.

Annie nodded.

'You were hardly expected,' said Aunt Hegarty.

'I am a niece!' said Annie.

'There are only six bunks!' cried Rose warningly.

'One person has to keep watch! Do let her come!' pleaded Emma. The others agreed, though they thought Annie was a nuisance, turning up at this stage.

'Very well,' said Aunt Hegarty, going out to telegraph the orphanage. The others sat down to give Annie tea.

That night she shared Emma's bed. When Emma woke up in the morning she was nearly on the floor and Annie had all the bedclothes.

'Did you kick other people out of bed at the orphanage?' Emma grumbled.

'No,' Annie said. 'At the orphanage we slept three in a bed and I was in the middle, there wasn't room to kick at all.'

They left for the boat directly after breakfast and, once on board, lost little time in stowing away their things.

Mr Mumpus had been wheeling his barrow between the house and the dock since early dawn, and on the last journey, he dumped a wicker crate on the dock. It contained two of his carrier pigeons, which as a pigeon fancier he bred himself.

'Seeing as you may be out of reach of a telegraph office, miss,' he explained to Emma, 'and Miss Hegarty may want to get in touch with Bella and me, if it's only to get the beds aired for your coming home. The black one, Paradise Percy, he's the fastest. But if you want to be certain the message arrives, send the white one, Queener Sheba. She'll come back to me if she drops a-dead in doing it.'

'Oh, I do hope she won't do that!' said Emma.

While Lucy ran down to the engine-room to start up the engines Emma hung up the cage of pigeons and buttered the kitten's feet for fear it should try to jump overboard and swim ashore, till the goat, tied to the back of the wheelhouse, bleated to have its feet buttered too.

The *Happy-Go-Gay* began slowly to reverse, her engines chugging, while Aunt Hegarty steered a careful course down

the dock and the nieces crowded on the rails to wave good-bye to Bella and Mr Mumpus who were holding their handkerchiefs to their eyes and sobbing as they kissed their hands and waved.

'Why do people always cry when they see ships go out to sea?' Harriet asked curiously.

'It's something to do with Eternal-Father-Strong-to-Save. I feel it myself!' said Emma, bursting into tears and flinging her arms round the nanny goat's neck, till Aunt Hegarty called her into the wheelhouse to take a spell at the wheel.

Chapter Five

Annie

Sophie was the cook. She liked it and cooking for numbers did not worry her. Harriet was her cook's boy.

Emma took care of the animals and Rose had volunteered to scrub the deck since Lucy was in the engine-room.

They asked Annie what she would like to do. As a stranger and an orphan they felt bound to be kind to her, and to treat her as a guest. Annie cast down her eyes and said nothing. The other nieces were about to suggest that she made the bunks in the morning, laid the meals and ran errands, when she said suddenly:

'I should like to help in the kitchen.'

'But Harriet helps in the kitchen!' Sophie said kindly. Harriet said nothing, but she said it very loudly. The others thought Annie was being tiresome but that Harriet was being a pig.

'Can't I help as well?' said Annie determinedly.

'Well – there's all the vegetables to sort and the stores are not properly put away yet,' said Sophie. 'You could do that while we are cooking the dinner.'

Annie's eyes grew bright with pleasure. She came into the cook's galley wearing her thick orphanage cloak.

'You won't want that in here!' said Sophie kindly. 'It's *hot*!'

Annie took no notice of what Sophie said. With her serge cloak still buttoned up to the chin she set to work putting away the stores in the tins marked Flour, Tea, Sugar and Cocoa.

Harriet carried the potatoes out on to the deck to peel while Sophie began to make a roly-poly pudding. Presently she came to fetch some raisins from the stores bag. To her shocked surprise Annie had already opened the bag and Sophie was quite positive she had been putting some in the pocket under her cloak. She looked very red when Sophie took away the bag without saying a word.

After dinner the last piece of roly-poly pudding disappeared in a twinkling when Annie was helping to wash the dishes.

'But where can it be? Where *can* it be?' Sophie kept saying, for one moment it had been there and the next moment – gone. Annie just bent over the dishes and said nothing.

'She took it I saw her!' Harriet whispered to Sophie. 'I saw her take it out of the plate and put it under her cloak.'

Sophie did the most sensible thing possible under the circumstances. She went straight to tell Aunt Hegarty.

The *Happy-Go-Gay* was steaming down the Channel at a splendid rate with a stream of smoke issuing from her smoke-stack. She was rolling ever so little, with a clank like an old bucket, but it was a pleasant noise, and Aunt Hegarty, standing at the wheel, seemed well satisfied with her new ship and her crew. She smiled very kindly down at Sophie.

'Well Sophie! You provided us with an excellent dinner!' said Aunt Hegarty. 'Would you like to take the wheel?'

'If you please Aunt Hegarty, our cousin Annie is stealing the food,' said Sophie.

'Then she had better not work in the kitchen!' said Aunt Hegarty. 'Some people can't keep their fingers out of things, it's pick, pick, pick the whole time! But if she really is hungry give her a piece of cake and send her to me.'

When Sophie returned to the kitchen Harriet met her with a scandalized expression. 'She *would* go in the larder!' she said, 'I couldn't stop her! She's in there *now*!'

Sophie marched into the larder and found Annie with both her hands full of cake.

'You are to go to Aunt Hegarty at *once*!' she said.

Annie thrust the cake underneath her cloak and flew up the stairs to the wheelroom.

'What's all this about your stealing food?' said Aunt Hegarty. 'Are you hungry?'

'I need a lot of food!' said Annie with a kind of desperation.

'I daresay you're right. You are thin enough!' said Aunt Hegarty. 'But you can't go helping yourself like that. We are on a voyage you know, and we can only take so much with us. Those provisions have to last seven people until we come home again.'

'There's enough for eight or nine people!' Annie protested.

'Possibly!' said Aunt Hegarty. 'But there may be emergencies. If there is any more trouble I shall have to turn back and put you ashore. Now go down into the engine-room and help Lucy clean the boilers.'

Annie's face brightened and she almost skipped towards the engine-room ladder. At the last moment she turned back and said:

'Aunt?'

'Yes, Annie?'

'How long will it be before it is too far to turn round and go home?' asked Annie.

'The point of no return will be midday tomorrow, Thursday July the 18th, in the year of Our Lord, eighteen hundred and seventy,' said Aunt Hegarty. 'But after that any trouble is punishable by court martial.'

'Yes Aunt!' said Annie, disappearing.

Lucy was not wholly pleased to see Annie arrive. She had enjoyed reigning supreme in her new kingdom, which was beginning to shine with the care and attention she gave it. Sophie had brought her a nice little lunch, beautifully served on a wooden tray. Lucy had carefully wiped her dirty hands before sitting down to enjoy it, with the *Happy-Go-Gay*'s heartbeats throbbing cheerfully in her ears. Life, felt Lucy, could not hold anything more romantic than her mechanical world below deck, and now here came Annie.

'I'm to help you polish!' said Annie.

'It's all clean!' said Lucy, looking jealously at her shining boilers.

'Aunt Hegarty said I was to,' said Annie, her face pink and shiny from the heat of the engine-room and the thickness of her cloak.

'You can sweep the floor if you like!' said Lucy.

Annie swept the floor half-heartedly. Beyond the few crumbs from Lucy's lunch there was not very much to sweep.

'Isn't there anything more interesting to do?' said Annie.

'Not really!' said Lucy, greasing some rods. 'We shall need some more coal in a minute.'

'From the hold?' said Annie excitedly. 'I'll get it.'

She seized the coal bucket and disappeared in the direction of the hold. Lucy finished her greasing but Annie did not come back. It was more peaceful being without her but the boiler fire was getting low. Lucy walked towards the door opening on to the ladder that led to the hold.

When she opened the door a strange sound met her ears.

It was the sound of sobbing.

Chapter Six

In the Engine-Room

Lucy stood shocked.

Had Annie fallen down the ladder?

Or was she feeling lost and homesick, and just enjoying a good cry in the dark? Lucy's conscience pricked her. She had been ungracious to Annie, she had not been pleased to see her come into the engine-room, and Annie, an orphan and a stranger, had felt unwanted.

'Annie!' she called softly, 'Annie!'

The sobbing stopped suddenly.

There was a pause, then Annie's voice called: 'Yes, Lucy! I'm coming!'

Lucy could hear her groping her way across the hold. Annie said something else but she did not catch it. It sounded like 'Do be patient!'

'It's all right!' Lucy called, 'I just wondered where you were. Did you hurt yourself or anything?'

'No!' said Annie, panting up the ladder. Her white face peered up at Lucy, blinking at the light. Her eyes were dry. Perhaps she had not been crying for very long.

'Where's the bucket?' said Lucy.

'The bucket?' said Annie. 'Oh, the bucket! Can I have a lantern?' she asked suddenly. 'I can't see the coal!'

'I'll fetch it!' said Lucy, bringing the lantern, but Annie snatched it almost rudely out of her hand and scrambled back down the ladder to the hold.

Lucy returned to her engines. She was just getting impatient again when Annie returned with the coal.

'Where's the lantern?' Lucy asked.

'The lantern?' said Annie. 'Oh! I left it down there hanging on a nail so I can find my way next time I go down and get the coal.'

Lucy was vexed but she did not want to scold Annie. She shovelled coal into the boiler with sharp angry pushes till the pulsing of the engines soothed her nerves.

Sophie brought in a cup of tea and they strolled on to the afterdeck to enjoy some fresh air.

They were out of sight of land now.

A few seagulls following like small kites flown on invisible strings were already preparing to leave them, and an apricot tint in the western sky caught the tops of the waves with the early glow of a summer evening.

Something moved beneath their feet. There was a scuttle and a shuffling noise.

'Aunt Hegarty said there weren't any rats in the hold!' Sophie said. 'Well I believe there are!'

'Annie was down there just now. She didn't say anything about rats!' said Lucy. 'I thought she was crying there but she wasn't much. Do you like her, Sophie?'

'She's our cousin and her parents are dead. We've got to like her,' said Sophie.

The scuttling sound came again.

'Emma's kitten had better go down and have a look round!' said Sophie, going away to find Emma.

'Let me take it down!' begged Annie when Emma carried the kitten into the hold.

Nobody else was very anxious to go down in the dark if there really were rats in the hold, so they let Annie go down the ladder with the kitten in her arms. Emma had christened it Captain Bligh.

Night fell and Aunt Hegarty said the kitten was to sleep in the hold. The rest took a bunk each, leaving Lucy at the wheel for the first watch. After a day below decks she was glad to feel the fresh night breeze on her cheeks and to plot her course by compass and the bright stars hanging above her in the heavens. Beneath her feet the engine chugged out its happy rhythm, and Lucy's heart throbbed joyously in unison. This is the life! thought Lucy. If I could live happy-ever-after in a steam-boat I'd never even want a birthday any more.

And then, to shatter her content, the sound of sobbing struck her ears once more, not very near but not very far away. Somewhere in the ship some member of the crew was breaking its heart where Lucy was rejoicing. How unfair life could be!

Lucy set the wheel on course as Aunt Hegarty had showed her how to do and peeped into the bunk-room prepared to comfort the sorrower, but everything was still. In the Captain's room Aunt Hegarty lay on her back, snoring like a master mariner, putting in a couple of hours rest before relieving Lucy at the wheel. Lucy returned to stand beside Annie's bunk, looking down at her. Perhaps she was sobbing in her dreams? But Annie's black lashes lay quiet on her pale cheeks, one hand was tucked under her face and the other rested on the hairy blanket outside. Far, far away from Lucy, Annie's dreams were quiet and undismayed. Her breast moved rhythmically in peaceful breathing.

Lucy went back to her post unsatisfied, but the sobbing was stilled.

Perhaps after all it was just the kitten, chasing the rats down in the hold.

Chapter Seven

In the Hold

The morning air brought secrets from more distant oceans. Gone were the fog-bound coasts, the grey-green seas, the sullen skies, the white cliffs and the small seaside towns babbling along the shores of home.

Riding the breeze, mysterious flavours wafted by, the tang of salt was tinged with mystery, and the tumbling clouds were madder, merrier than the clouds they knew, pelting across a sky the colour of a kingfisher's crown.

The nieces tumbled on to the deck, yawning and chattering, roused by the delightful smell of bacon that Sophie was cooking for them in the galley.

Emma had milked the goat and frothing bowlfuls waited on the table. 'I must fetch Captain Bligh for his breakfast!' she said.

'*I* will fetch Captain Bligh for his breakfast!' cried Annie, hurling herself past Emma with a bowl of milk in one hand and a slice of bread and bacon in the other. Bad manners in such close quarters could not pass unnoticed and the nieces exchanged disapproving glances as Annie hurtled by. Nobody said a word however. They knew it was unkind to refer to Annie's orphanage upbringing and allowances must be made, but really, she was very provoking.

There was a marked coldness when their cousin returned cuddling the cat.

'Did it catch any rats?' Harriet asked at last.

'I don't know!' said Annie, fondling Captain Bligh. 'I didn't see any.'

'You have left your mug behind!' pointed out Rose.

Annie said nothing at all.

'Well, you'll have to wash it up, later, for yourself!' said Sophie. Annie just tossed her head.

Suddenly a suspicion shot through Lucy's head. She stared hard at Annie, thinking deeply, remembering what had happened yesterday and how Annie had behaved, and slowly the suspicion became a certainty. She said nothing until they were back in the engine-room, and then:

'*I* am going to fetch the coal from the hold today!' said Lucy.

'No, I will!' said Annie, jumping for the bucket.

'I will!' said Lucy firmly.

'Oh do let me, Lucy! Please do!' pleaded Annie piteously.

'Why?' said Lucy sternly, 'You can't enjoy going down into that stuffy dark hold.'

'I do! I do!' said Annie.

'I don't believe it!' said Lucy. 'And anyway it is *my* engine-room and *my* boilers and *I'm* going. Give me the lantern!'

Annie did a surprising thing. She reached sullenly for the lantern hanging above her head and then deliberately dropped it on the floor. The lantern smassed into pieces.

'Oh you clumsy thing!' cried Lucy in anger.

The lantern would have to be repaired. Meanwhile Lucy took with her a box of wax matches and prepared to enter the hold. All of a sudden her heart began to beat very fast.

'Please don't go, Lucy! Oh please don't! *Please, please!*' she begged, but Lucy brushed her aside. As she opened the door and stepped on to the ladder a scratching scuffling noise below sent cold shivers down her spine, but she climbed on, and then, as she reached the bottom of the ladder, came a bang that reverberated through the ship.

Over her head Annie had shut the door with a crash and Lucy could hear her dragging something heavy across the trap. She was shut in below with whatever it was Annie didn't want her to see.

Lucy let the echoes die away, and then she listened. There was nothing to be heard but the throbbing of the engines overhead, no sobbing, no rustling, no movement of any kind. But the beating of her heart seemed to hammer louder than the engines, and she kept her eyes fixed on the tiny crack of light round the trapdoor, hardly daring to peer into the darkness all around her.

Again she listened and listened.

Now Annie was marching to and fro across the engine-room floor above, and singing, in a loud defiant voice. Whenever she crossed the trapdoor she stamped on it and the trap rang with a dreadful clatter that reverberated through Lucy's head.

The words Annie was singing were very odd:

'Don't stir!
Don't stir!
It's only her!
It's only her!
Sit tight!
She's got no light!
If you don't make a sound you'll be all right!
Don't shout!
Don't come out!
Nobody's going to find you out!'

The words made a shiver creep up and down Lucy's spine as she realized her suspicions were well founded.

Somewhere down there in the darkness somebody was hidden. She was shut in the hold with a stranger that Annie knew about. Who could it be, or what?

Anything was better than just listening in the dark.

'Are you there?' she whispered during a pause in the singing. 'I'm Lucy! Who are you?'

No answer came. Just the faintest rustling and more stamps on the trap above.

'I'm going to strike a match!' Lucy said with her teeth chattering. 'I've got some in my pocket.'

This time there was a definite rustle as if legs and arms were being drawn up out of sight in a far corner of the hold. It was a frightened kind of noise and it put courage into Lucy. She struck her first match which fizzled and went out. She was striking a second when a voice from the corner made her jump and the box fell out of her hands. It was a hoarse voice and fear had made it savage.

'If you does that again,' said the threatening voice, 'I'll get a lump of coal and bash your head in!'

Lucy's knees turned to water. She dared not even stop to pick up the box of matches. Her teeth began to chatter.

'Who are you?' she whispered.

There was no reply.

'I'm not – going – to – hurt – you!' said Lucy. 'Just – just – tell – me – who – you – are!'

Still no answer came, but there was a scraping sound as if somebody really was picking up a lump of coal to throw at her head. This was too much for Lucy. The thought that someone might be looking at her in the dark, where she could see nothing at all, sent her scampering back to the ladder to pound with her fists on the closed trap, beseeching at the top of her voice: 'Annie! Annie! Let me out! Let me out!'

The footsteps paused, and then a strange thing happened. Another pair of feet, heavier and more determined than Annie's, entered the boiler-room above, and Aunt Hegarty's voice exclaimed:

'If you must sing, Annie, sing in tune. And where is Lucy?'

Lucy's pounding fists answered her question, and barely was the trapdoor open before she was through it and pointing back into the darkness with a trembling finger.

'Aunt Hegarty! Aunt Hegarty! There is a stowaway in the hold!'

Chapter Eight

Stowaways

It was Annie's turn to tremble.

From stamping and threatening and singing she became a small cringing shadow, her face as white as paint. Her mouth opened and shut, but not a word passed her lips as her eyes fixed themselves on Aunt Hegarty.

Lucy expected Aunt Hegarty to plunge immediately into the hold, but she did not.

Instead she pointed sternly to Annie.

'Tell whoever it is to come out immediately!' she ordered.

Meekly, Annie knelt at the trapdoor and called down in a small hoarse voice:

'You're to come out now!'

A shuffling of feet could be heard among the coal. Then came tentative steps on the ladder, and presently a face shrouded in an orphanage cloak, black with coal but streaked white in places with tears, peeped over the edge of the trapdoor. The figure, filthy with coal dust, was just staggering to its feet when close on its heels an identical face, also black and tear-stained, popped into view. Another cloaked figure stumbled across the trap, and Aunt Hegarty paused to peer down the ladder for further revelations before demanding in her harshest tones:

'And *who are you*?'

Both the figures immediately covered their dirty faces with their cloaks and broke into bitter sobbing.

Annie sprang in front of them with her arms outstretched,

like a mother hen defending her young. Small as she was her spare little body shielded them.

Lucy saw a kind of light dart from her eyes as she challenged Aunt Hegarty, as if everything that she possessed was now at stake.

'They're my sisters!' she cried passionately.

After a pause, Aunt Hegarty said more gently,

'And why were they hidden as stowaways in the hold?'

'You wouldn't have taken them with you!' Annie's hoarse voice pursued. 'And I couldn't come without them!'

'They need a bath,' said Aunt Hegarty. 'And some clean clothes, and I daresay some breakfast. Annie! Come to me in the wheelhouse directly. Lucy! Take these two to Sophie and tell her to bath and feed them. I will see them later.'

She stalked out of the engine-room, followed reluctantly by Annie, who cast piteous looks over her shoulder at the two dirty little stowaways being shepherded into the cook's galley by Lucy.

Once Lucy had delivered them she was thankful to return to her engines, almost overwhelmed by the excitement of the last short half-hour. She spent the next fifty minutes stoking, polishing, sweeping and cleaning, as if to make up to her boilers for the neglect they had been forced to endure.

It must be admitted that she was rather pleased about the stowaways. It was she, after all, who had discovered them and it gave a kind of status to the voyage.

Meanwhile Aunt Hegarty had just delivered a long lecture to Annie on deceit and subterfuge, and had sent her to the cabin in tears.

Aunt Hegarty was plotting her new course for the day when suddenly Sophie appeared at the wheelhouse door with an anxious expression on her face. 'Please Aunt Hegarty,' she said apologetically, 'I'm afraid both the stowaways are boys!'

Chapter Nine

Court Martial

'There must be a Court Martial,' said Aunt Hegarty. 'First of Annie, and then the stowaways. It will be easier to do them all together. In each case the prisoner may have a Friend to speak for him.'

It was taken for granted that Annie would act as Prisoner's Friend for her brothers. The question was, who would be Annie's Friend? Lucy knew she ought to offer, but the morning had been a bit much and Aunt Hegarty abruptly settled it by calling her as witness for the prosecution.

Emma said she would like to be Prisoner's Friend and sat next to Annie, holding her hand.

Aunt Hegarty, of course, was in the chair.

Annie was charged on three counts.

(1) For concealing stowaways on board.
(2) For bringing Boys on to the *Happy-Go-Gay*.
(3) For telling lies about it.

'The last two charges are by far the most serious,' said Aunt Hegarty. 'Does the prisoner plead guilty or not guilty?'

'Guilty,' said Annie.

'In that case we have only to decide on the punishment,' said Aunt Hegarty severely. 'Has the Prisoner's Friend anything to say in her defence?'

'Please Aunt Hegarty, she can't help having brothers!' said Emma.

'You all have brothers,' Aunt Hegarty remarked, 'I didn't

notice your bringing any of them on board as stowaways.'

'Please Aunt Hegarty our brothers have a mother and a father!' said Emma. 'They have a much better time than we do! We didn't mind leaving them behind.'

'I see,' said Aunt Hegarty. 'But the prisoner lied about it.'

'Couldn't you punish her for the lie and forgive the other charges?' Emma pleaded. Annie's fingers grew tight round her arm.

'We had better vote on that,' said Aunt Hegarty.

After a vote the rest of the nieces agreed that Annie should be punished on Count Three and severely reprimanded on both the other counts.

'The punishment will be decided later,' said Aunt Hegarty. 'Meanwhile proceed with the trial of the other prisoners.'

Still pale, Annie moved over to sit beside her brothers, who had long since ceased crying, and, wrapped in blankets, were hiccoughing, partly from fear and partly from the effects of the hearty breakfast Sophie had given them. Stripped of their orphanage cloaks, brushed, combed and washed, they were unmistakably boys, small, beetle-browed, and with something of Annie's determination about their round scrubbed faces.

'State the prisoners' names,' ordered Aunt Hegarty.

'Charleyboy and Gustus,' said Annie.

'State how they came to stow away in the hold of my ship,' said Aunt Hegarty.

'They ran away from the orphanage with me,' Annie said in a small frightened voice. 'I borrowed the other orphans' cloaks to keep them warm. I hid them down in the hold before I came to your house. They've been there ever since.'

'They were fed with food stolen from the ship's provisions,' Aunt Hegarty said.

'Yes,' said Annie.

'Did they know that, if discovered, they would immediately be turned off the ship?' said Aunt Hegarty.

'Yes,' said Annie.

'And that this voyage is restricted to girls, so that not only were they stowaways but also Usurpers?' said Aunt Hegarty.

'Yes,' said Annie.

'Do you plead guilty to these charges?' Aunt Hegarty demanded of the two little boys.

Both nodded their heads, too overcome to speak.

'Has the Prisoner's Friend anything to say on their behalf?' Aunt Hegarty asked Annie.

'Please Ma'am it was all my fault!' said Annie, 'they would never have thought of it themselves. They didn't like being in the hold at all.'

'Well, there is very little more I can add,' said Aunt Hegarty. 'Your conduct, Annie, has been most reprehensible and unworthy of a niece of mine. As for your brothers, stowaways never have any conduct and besides, they must be got rid of immediately.'

The little boys broke into a wail.

Annie managed to restrain her tears in order to stammer, 'Please Ma'am – how?'

Sophie, Harriet, Rose, Emma and Lucy had dreadful visions of the stowaways being made to walk the plank.

'We must put back and land them at once,' said Aunt Hegarty. 'Fortunately the orphanage knows where you are, Annie, and will no doubt put two and two together. You will all return there when we dock. I should not dream of including you in the voyage, Annie, after this affair. That must be your punishment.'

Annie and the stowaways were all crying now. At that moment the watch sounded the midday bells. At once Annie raised her head in one last defiant gesture.

'That is – that is the Point of No Return!' sniffed Annie.

Aunt Hegarty feverishly studied her chart. Her lips closed and her face became at once resigned and grim. Slowly she nodded her head.

'It is quite true. We cannot go back now,' she pronounced.

The Court was very quiet.

Emma could bear it no longer.

'Then we can take them with us?' she cried.

'Of course not,' said Aunt Hegarty. 'They are *Boys*. We shall have to think of something else to do with them.'

'There is the lifeboat!' said Harriet. 'We could give them provisions and things . . .'

'And set them ashore on a desert island,' said Rose.

The little boys stopped crying and looked hopeful.

'For the present we will keep that in mind,' said Aunt Hegarty. 'Please watch for a desert island. Meanwhile, bread and water for all three of them.'

'Where are they to sleep?' Sophie inquired, thinking of the crowded cabin.

'In the hold of course!' snapped Aunt Hegarty. 'They have slept there before!'

Charleyboy and Gustus broke into a howl. Sophie looked troubled.

'It's the washing! They get so very dirty!' she protested. 'I've only just washed their shirts and those awful cloaks . . .'

'Then they can sleep on the seats on the deck,' Aunt Hegarty ordered, and there the matter ended.

Chapter Ten

The Storm

When all hands came on deck the next morning they found everything clean swept and tidy. The decks had been washed down, the rails polished, buckets of coal provided for the engine-room, the goat's bed changed and fresh straw added, drinking water pumped and ropes neatly coiled where they ought to lie. Annie was sitting in the sun, mending shirts. Her brothers, having finished the deck work, greeted Aunt Hegarty with a smart salute which she acknowledged, but did not speak, to them.

Quite unperturbed Charleyboy and Gustus trotted away to inspect the fishing-lines with which they were fishing over the side of the boat. Everybody breakfasted on fresh dabs fried by Sophie in batter, except Annie, who ate bread and water at the table, and her brothers who were not invited to join the crew in the saloon.

Rose pushed a piece of dab towards Annie, who sat beside her. Everyone felt so uncomfortable enjoying the fish without her. Annie had a way of eating bread and water that made everyone else feel guilty, but she shook her head violently at Rose's offer.

The little boys worked all day. When they were not polishing Aunt Hegarty's telescope they were splicing ropes. When there were no more ropes to be spliced they took soundings, made fish hooks, groomed the goat and peeled potatoes.

Punctually at meal times they sounded the ship's bell, then queued up for the mugs of water and slices of bread that Sophie doled out to them, and trotted away to eat them behind the smokestack. They made funny little bows whenever the nieces spoke to them, but every time Aunt Hegarty passed they drew themselves up very straight and saluted.

'They're our *cousins*!' Emma whispered to Harriet. 'If our brothers were here they would all play together. It seems funny to be treating them like stowaways.'

'But they *are* stowaways!' said Harriet.

All the same, on the second day Sophie put dripping on their bread and handed it to them upside down. If Aunt Hegarty noticed them wiping their fingers down the sides of their pantaloons she did not say anything about it.

When Charleyboy and Gustus found Rose scrubbing the deck they took the bucket from her and scrubbed it themselves. Aunt Hegarty called Rose to her cabin and gave her the logbook to write up. Rose had beautiful handwriting. She also had the accounts to do and became a kind of secretary to Aunt Hegarty.

Annie was much more cheerful now and made herself useful in a number of ways. She kept a motherly eye on her little brothers and ordered them about very loudly as often as possible. Three days went by very quickly, and then Harriet, who was on look-out duty, saw a desert island.

She made quite certain, before announcing it, by taking a long look through Aunt Hegarty's telescope.

'Island ahoy! Desert island ahoy oh!' shouted Harriet.

Everyone came pouring on deck to crowd on the rail. Aunt Hegarty strode out of the wheelhouse, leaving the wheel to Rose. The little boys began to leap up and down, forgetting to salute. Only Annie did not seem at all pleased about seeing the island.

'It's *our* island! It's our desert island! It's *ours*!' shouted Charleyboy and Gustus, turning cartwheels down the deck. Then they raced away to collect their fishing-lines and the cloaks, now clean and dry, that they had brought with them from the orphanage. Their bundle of possessions seemed pitifully small.

'Shall we let down the lifeboat, Ma'am?' they asked respectfully, saluting Aunt Hegarty.

'Crew to man the lifeboat!' commanded Aunt Hegarty.

Lucy, Rose, Emma and the boys immediately began to loose the boat from her davits.

'They must take a certain amount of provisions with them,' Aunt Hegarty said. 'Sophie, I leave that to you.'

When the boat was ready and Sophie had prepared a generous basket of food for the castaways Annie stood beside her brothers, prepared to embark with them on the journey ashore.

'You are not going too?' said Emma.

'Yes I am!' said Annie.

'No, she's not!' cried the ungrateful boys. 'We don't want her!'

'She pushes us about!' said Charleyboy.

'She tells us what to do!' said Gustus.

'We want the island for ourselves!' they both repeated. 'It is an island just for *boys* to live on.'

The nieces were perplexed, and sorry for Annie.

'Stay with us, Annie!' Sophie said. 'We shall pick them up again on our way home.'

But Annie and her brothers continued to argue until finally Aunt Hegarty went back to the wheelhouse and left them to settle it among themselves.

Nobody noticed the black clouds rolling up the sky, which should have been Harriet's business to see as look-out.

Suddenly the sun went in, pushed behind the clouds by an inky finger. An icy ripple swept the sea, and in its wake dark swollen waves beat against the steamer's sides and began to push and buffet her towards the shore.

'Full steam ahead! We'll be on the reef!' Aunt Hegarty cried from the wheelhouse. 'See to your engines, Lucy! Haul up the lifeboat, Rose and Emma! Tie everything down, Sophie and Harriet and Annie – we are in for a storm!'

Within moments the uneasy, swelling sea had become a boiling pot where waves burst one white top against another, and spouted crests of foam. Soon the desert island was framed in spray tossed off the treacherous reef.

Lucy's sturdy engines thundered into action. The *Happy-Go-Gay* turned away from danger and headed south by east, leaving the land veiled in a mist that slowly swallowed up the palm trees.

Disappointed, the little boys dropped their bundles, and then rushed to help secure the lifeboat and to brace their legs against the new heaving of the deck.

Held firmly on her course by the iron hand of Aunt Hegarty the *Happy-Go-Gay* pitched and tossed in the storm.

At one moment she seemed up-ended like a duck, exploring with its head, the depths below the waves. At the next, she bobbed up again to wallow from side to side as if anxious to shake the water off her decks. Then with a frantic wriggle she plunged sideways, with a groan and a heave, till many a time Lucy, keeping her engines throttled down, fancied that the ship was breaking in half, to leave her islanded beside her boilers, afloat amid the turbulence around her.

For a while the task of stoking and keeping the engines in order distracted her attention, but before long the dreadful pangs of seasickness made themselves felt and Lucy wondered

how long she could survive this battering. Annie should be there to help her, but no Annie came to her call, and Lucy's head ached, while a great drowsiness stole over her as she longed above everything else to creep into her bunk and lie down.

Coal was needed from the hold, but Lucy knew she would use the very last lump before descending into the surging darkness to fill the bucket.

Somewhere she could hear the slap, slap of the bilge water slopping up and down. Either the *Happy-Go-Gay* was leaking or the sea water breaking over her decks was unable to get away. Somebody ought to see to the pumps.

Aunt Hegarty's hands must be full in keeping the ship on her course, while Lucy dared not leave her engines except to look for coal.

'Annie!' she shouted, 'Annie! Annie!'

No Annie appeared, but the door of the engine-room opened and Gustus and Charleyboy crept inside.

'Annie's sick!' said Charleyboy, 'so is Rose and so is Sophie and so is Emma.'

'So is Harriet!' added Gustus, 'but not the Adm'ral, and not the goat either. Did you want a cup of tea?'

'*Yes!* No!' cried Lucy frantically, 'I've got no coal for the boiler, and somebody ought to man the pumps – quickly!'

The next moment Gustus was down the ladder with the coal bucket, while Charleyboy was working the pump handle to and fro to the tune of a cheerful shanty.

'You look shockin'ly green, Cousin Lucy!' he said cheerfully. 'Are you sick too?'

Lucy could only nod. Fortunately Gustus arriving that moment with the coal diverted her attention from the queasiness of her stomach. And a few minutes later a cup of tea was thrust into her hands by fingers still black with coal dust, but kind and businesslike and attentive.

'I made it, miss!' Gustus said proudly. 'The Admiral had one too. Everyone else was too sick. I milked the goat too. One time it was just like as if it was standing on its head and I was milking it upside down.'

'You haven't got to call me Miss!' said Lucy, gratefully swallowing the scalding tea. 'I'm your cousin Lucy.'

'We're stowaways, miss! and we want to be castaways next!' replied Gustus promptly. 'We don't want to stop on a ship full of girls. If it hadn't been for that mutt Annie we'd have been on the desert island by now!'

'If it hadn't been for your sister Annie you would still have been in the orphanage,' said Lucy severely.

'We liked the orphanage! We all did!' said the boys together. 'Annie only came away because she was jealous and wanted to be a niece as well and Charleyboy and I wanted to be castaways. We didn't want to be shut up in a ship full of girls. We're going to get off it just as quick as we can.'

'Oh well, I expect there will be another desert island quite soon,' said Lucy, turning her back on him and wishing that the cup of tea had made her feel better instead of worse.

'You look green all over, even your hair!' said Gustus kindly. 'Look! Charleyboy and me will look after the engines while you go and lie down, like the others. Just a little while, cousin Lucy! It will do you good! There's nothing can go wrong. If it does we'll come and call you!'

Thankfully, Lucy fled to her bunk and lay there listening to the beat of the pump, manned by Charleyboy, and the drone of a sea-shanty sung by Gustus who really had no idea of the tune.

Chapter Eleven

A Birthday Message

Lucy awoke to a delightful feeling of peace. Her bunk which had been trying to tip her out all night was now still, and the faint vibration of her engines below soothed her like the quiet purring of a pet cat.

Too drowsy to remember the events of the previous day, Lucy turned over, and was about to close her eyes once more when Sophie appeared beside her, carrying a plate of bread and butter.

'Would you like some breakfast?' Sophie asked. 'We have all had ours. Aunt Hegarty said you were to rest, because of working so hard all day yesterday in the storm.'

Lucy bounced up in bed.

'My engines!' she cried. 'What has become of my engines?'

'Gustus is stoking and Charleyboy is polishing something with a rag,' said Sophie. 'Aunt Hegarty is in the wheelhouse, Emma has milked the goat, Harriet is making a rice pudding, Annie is sweeping the deck and Rose is counting out the rations. A lot of the bags got spoiled by the storm when the waves came into the locker. We are getting very short of food, especially since Aunt Hegarty said the boys can be on full rations, like the rest of us. So they have dropped some fishing-lines overboard and we hope they will catch some more fish.'

'What day is it?' said Lucy, scrambling out of bed.

'It is July the nineteenth, eighteen hundred and seventy . . .'

said Sophie and then stopped short and they both exclaimed together:

'It is dear Mamma's birthday and we have all of us forgotten about it!'

'Poor Mamma will think we have been drowned!' said Sophie when they told the other nieces.

'Mamma would rather we had been drowned than that we should forget her!' said Harriet reproachfully.

There was very little help for it. There they were in the middle of a wide ocean, not a post-card shop within sight, and no postage stamps. Lucy went soberly to her engine-room.

'You look very sad!' said Gustus and Charleyboy, who had

expected Lucy to be pleased with the way they had cherished her engines while she slept. 'Are you still feeling seasick?'

Lucy explained about the birthday.

'Why don't you send a message in a bottle like people always do at sea?' Charleyboy suggested.

'Quickly! Quickly go and tell the others!' Lucy exclaimed gratefully, taking over the engines from Gustus.

While Charleyboy spread the idea among the nieces, Gustus, with the help of the kitten, Captain Bligh, searched the hold for a bottle, and Rose wrote a birthday message in her beautiful copperplate handwriting.

Dear Mamma,

We are having a beautiful voyage in distant oceans. The *Happy-Go-Gay*, her Commander and all her crew are in good health. We hope that you and dear Papa and our brothers are well, and we wish you many returns of your birthday.

They all signed their names including Aunt Hegarty. But the two boys refused to sign.

'But everybody should sign!' urged Lucy.

'Not stowaways!' said Gustus proudly. So Rose wrote at the bottom of the letter, 'There are also two stowaways on board.'

'I do hope dear Mamma does not imagine that stowaways are dangerous!' murmured Rose sealing the envelope.

They dropped the bottle overboard, but it seemed to take an immense time falling back just the length of the ship.

'How long do you think it will be before it gets there?' Emma asked Aunt Hegarty, watching the bobbing bottle.

'About six months I should think. It depends on the tide,' said Aunt Hegarty.

'Six months!' shrieked Emma. 'But dear Mamma's birthday is today! We shall have to send one of Mr Mumpus's pigeons!'

'Mr Mumpus's pigeons are for emergencies,' said Aunt Hegarty severely.

'This *is* an emergency!' wailed Emma.

'Well I suppose it is,' agreed Aunt Hegarty. 'But the time may come when the carrier pigeons are the only lifeline we have. It is a pity you did not think of it before. Very well, we will send a pigeon. It is fortunate we have two. Rose had better write another letter.'

The second letter was written in great haste. When it had been signed and sealed Emma tied it underneath the wing of Paradise Percy, the fastest of the pigeons. They knew that the moment it arrived at its own dovecot Mr Mumpus would send the letter to its destination.

All the nieces watched the pigeon winging its way from the ship's rail in the direction of home, and for the space of a minute their hearts travelled with it, until an announcement made by Aunt Hegarty from the wheelhouse pulled them back to the immediate present with a violent jerk.

'Do not be unduly disturbed, my dears,' Aunt Hegarty called through her megaphone. 'But Annie says there is a large pirate ship creeping up on us from behind.'

Chapter Twelve

The Pirate Ship

It would be hard to say which were the more astounded, the crew of the *Happy-Go-Gay* or the crew of the pirate ship.

On both vessels everybody immediately crowded to look over the rails. Aunt Hegarty appeared with her telescope, wearing her admiral's hat.

Now that the brigantine was actually towering above their heads the little boys seemed over-awed, and cowered beside the smokestack, peeping at the pirates from behind their fists.

'Shall I get up full steam?' Lucy said, prepared to fly to her engines, but Aunt Hegarty prevented her. Already the brigantine's guns were being trained on the deck of the *Happy-Go-Gay*, and if it came to another chase, the wind, now blowing strongly, was all in the pirates' favour.

As the sun leaped over the eastern horizon a boat was lowered from the brigantine, and four lusty oarsmen wearing black knitted caps began to row towards them. In the bows sat a dashing personality who could only be the Captain himself, an elegant if swarthy figure, decked out with lace ruffles, buckled shoes, silver cutlass, flashing rings, and a pair of black moustaches even more impressive than dear Papa's.

'Do not be so anxious,' Aunt Hegarty said to calm her trembling nieces. 'Pirates will hardly fire on women unless provoked. And we have practically nothing they will care to capture. Control your feelings and show dignity, even if you feel afraid.'

The nieces tried to obey Aunt Hegarty's instructions, but it seemed an eternity before four of the fierce-looking buccaneers clambered on board, and the Captain greeted Aunt Hegarty with a sweeping bow.

'Your servant, Admiral Ma'am!' he announced with an ironic wave of his hand. 'I have the honour to make you all my prisoners!'

He snapped his fingers at one of his men, who at once strode into the wheelhouse and stood beside the wheel, an impassive pillar staring into space. A second pirate clattered down the ladder into the engine-room. Lucy gave a little moan as she saw him disappear from sight.

'Bring the cargo on deck!' the Captain ordered Charleyboy and Gustus.

The boys trotted away to the hold, and returned with the small collection of trinkets and knick-knacks Harriet had bought at the Penny Bazaar. The pirate Captain brushed them scornfully aside.

'What else is there?' he demanded.

'There is nothing more,' a third buccaneer announced.

He had followed Charleyboy and Gustus into the hold and even searched the bunk-room and the wheelhouse. 'Only a goat and a dove and a ship's cat,' he added, as if Emma's pets were scarcely worth the trouble of mentioning.

'No jewellery? No watches? No rings?' said the Captain impatiently.

'Sir, if your coarseness stoops to robbing women helpless to defend themselves, you may have my watch!' said Aunt Hegarty with icy scorn. 'It belonged to my great grandmamma. Pardon me that I have no ring. I am not married.'

The Captain did not accept the watch that Aunt Hegarty dangled coldly at the end of a long chain. He flushed a dark red and turned aside as if thinking.

'In that case, Madam Admiral, I shall be obliged to seize your ship,' he said finally.

'I hope you can sail her,' said Aunt Hegarty drily. 'We have no more fuel.'

'You leave me no alternative, Madam,' said the Captain with ill-concealed fury. 'I shall have to take hostages.'

For the first time the nieces saw Aunt Hegarty blanch, but only for a moment.

'Sir!' she said coldly. 'These innocent children are in my care. Their parents, though of comfortable means, are hardly rich. It is just possible that my own poor bones have a paltry value as an explorer and butterfly collector of a certain reputation. Therefore, if you will undertake to see these innocent children safely into port, I will stay as a hostage in your ship until suitable terms can be arranged by my lawyer, dealing through my Bank.'

The nieces began to sob, while at the same time the pirate bo'sun, who was in close attendance on his Captain standing at his elbow, cleared his throat and said hoarsely:

'The men don't like lady hostages, Cap'n. Think it's unlucky to have women on board. Near to mutiny last time we did it. Remember?'

'Then we will sink the ship and they can all walk the plank!' shouted the Captain, losing his temper and turning violently away from the sobbing nieces. 'Tell Jason to get a marlingspike under the deck and prise up a beam. And afterwards you can drive a hole in her bottom and let the water in.'

But before the pirate Jason could pick up the marlingspike, Charleyboy and Gustus had flown to the Captain's side and were standing one at either knee.

'Captain sir! We'll be hostages, sir! Gustus and me will!'

'We're stowaways, sir, Charleyboy and me are! We want to be pirates, we always did, sir!'

'Take us aboard sir! We'll cook and clean and scrub for you, Captain! Please take us, Captain, please!'

The boys were brimming with enthusiasm. The nieces, taking them for heroes, saw that in fact they were no longer in the least afraid of the pirates, whose swashbuckling manners and gorgeous dress had completely captured their fancy.

As the Captain considered their plea and finally assented, they drew themselves stiffly to attention and saluted.

'Can we walk the plank *first* please, Cap'n?' they asked.

The Captain burst into a roar of laughter in which his body-guard joined. He slapped both boys on the back and put his arms round their shoulders.

'Well crowed, my bonny cockerels!' he cried. 'Come on then! Back to the ship and you shall see what a gay life we lead under the Jolly Roger. Kiss your sisters good-bye, lads, and let's be off!'

The boys hung back, bashful at the thought of kissing their five cousins, but Annie, pale as a sheet, stepped forward and between them.

'I'm coming too!' she said.

'No you aren't!' cried the boys together.

'You'll not take them without me!' Annie threatened the Captain, clenching her fists.

'We don't want you!' shouted Charleyboy and Gustus, making a dash for the side of the *Happy-Go-Gay*. 'We don't want girls on our pirate ship!'

'There, there, little lady! We'll take care of your brothers!' said the Captain, following the boys. 'They won't come to any harm. Hark at 'em! They don't want to stay with their sisters! Boys will be boys, you know!'

Annie promptly rushed at him, kicking and scratching. As the laughing pirates dropped over the side, Aunt Hegarty kindly but firmly took her by the arm.

'Don't grieve, my dear. Your brothers have behaved like brave English gentlemen,' she said, following the diminishing figures of Gustus and Charleyboy, now bouncing happily in the stern of the pirate jollyboat. 'Don't you realize they have saved our lives? But for them we should all have walked the plank by now. When we get home we will arrange to pay the pirates a ransom and then you shall have your brothers back again.'

But glancing over the vast boundless sea as the pirate ship

put about and slowly dwindled to a smaller and smaller dot on the blue ocean, even Aunt Hegarty was asking herself how and when, with no fuel, and supplies of food and water fast running out, the crew of the *Happy-Go-Gay* would ever reach their home shores again.

Chapter Thirteen

The Island

'There is a breeze, and we have got a sort of sail!' said Emma.

'There are two deck-chairs left,' said Rose.

'And the boiler fire isn't quite out,' said Lucy.

They ran to take advantage of whatever wind and firing was left. Aunt Hegarty consulted her sextant.

'If we sail at ten knots an hour for eight hours we *might* find an island,' she said.

Harriet suddenly remembered yesterday's rice pudding still in the galley and it was remarkable how a little food put new heart into them all.

Even Annie recovered from the uttermost depths of her despair and seemed to realize that the sooner dry land was touched the sooner she was likely to find means of rescuing her brothers.

'At least they are happy!' Sophie comforted her.

'I don't want them to be happy with *pirates*!' returned Annie.

Slowly the wind filled the sail. A filter of smoke began to stain the pale blue morning sky. They began to steal away in the opposite direction to the pirate ship, and heavy-hearted as they were with the loss of the boys, new hope revived with the movement of the boat, and the pattern of the water slipping past the stern.

'At least we aren't all at the bottom of the sea and the *Happy-Go-Gay* as well,' said Harriet.

There was plenty to do.

Strange what a time it took to chop up a couple of deck-chairs, and how dangerous a task it seemed, when Charleyboy and Gustus had made so light of it. When Emma had cut a large hole in the deck, and sliced the heel off her boot, Aunt Hegarty took the axe away and did it herself. Even she was not so very good at it.

Annie and Rose scoured the hold till the last vestige of coal dust had been collected.

'You needn't get any more. It's no use burning cobwebs,' said Lucy.

But the wind maintained, the sail bellied out, and the little ferry steamer moved slowly but surely on her course with Aunt Hegarty's hand on the wheel, facing the unknown with a shipful of hope and so few provisions left that Sophie's hand trembled as she fingered the small paper packages of sugar and tea.

'I do hope there will be a shop on the island,' she said to Emma.

Even the goat was suffering from lack of enough water to drink. Every time it was milked it gave a little less. And nobody seemed able to catch fish like Charleyboy and Gustus.

'It's so *awful* without them,' said Annie.

The last of the fuel gave out.

Lucy came on deck to lean her elbows on the rails. Her task in the engine-room was finished.

'It's so lucky there is still some wind,' she said philosophically, watching their little sail still drawing the *Happy-Go-Gay* along at two knots an hour. It was all very quiet without the engines or Charleyboy and Gustus.

Suddenly Lucy raised her head from her arms and began to sniff the air like a dog.

'I can smell something lovely!' she said. 'Like coconut ice!'

They all sniffed the air.

'Coconuts!' said Sophie. 'And I can see something! Look, look! over there on the skyline, like little sticks – it's palm trees!'

'Oh!' said Rose. 'I thought for one dreadful moment it was another pirate ship!'

They all began to sing and dance. The palm trees grew clearer as they approached. A stronger smell of coconut wafted across the sea and a gorgeous butterfly, pink and bronze with bars and blotches of pure turquoise, fluttered over the water to perch on the side of the smokestack.

Rose darted away to fetch Aunt Hegarty's butterfly net, while Emma restrained the eager Captain Bligh from pouncing on the lovely creature.

'I thought so!' said Aunt Hegarty, when she had made a temporary prisoner of the butterfly. 'This specimen lives only in the Paradox Islands. I have never seen one alive before. We should be making a landfall before dark.'

'Are they nice islands?' asked Harriet.

'I believe they are very *rich* islands,' Aunt Hegarty said thoughtfully. 'We should be able to find plenty of coconuts for fuel, and some water and fruit. We must take in supplies as quickly as we can and get away.'

'Why?' asked the nieces. 'Why can't we stay there a week and bathe and have picnics?'

'The bathing is not very safe, there are sharks, I believe,' said Aunt Hegarty tartly.

'Well, picnics then?' said Rose. 'I would *so* like to sit down on the grass again!'

As Aunt Hegarty turned away to let the butterfly escape they all began to ask peevishly, 'Why can't we stay there a little while and have picnics, Aunt Hegarty?'

'The place has not got a very good reputation,' Aunt Hegarty replied evasively, and more than that she would not say.

As the sun went down the *Happy-Go-Gay* sailed into the island lagoon through a gap in the reef and floated into stiller water as the last of the breeze died out of her sails.

'Drop anchor quietly!' Aunt Hegarty ordered, and Lucy and Emma dropped the anchor overboard with a stately plop!

Aunt Hegarty had kept her telescope trained on the shore ever since the island was first sighted, and the nieces peered into the undergrowth bordering the graceful palm trees, watching for signs of life, for huts or tree-houses that might betray the haunts of savages, for boats or smoke signals showing that the island was not deserted.

No sign of life appeared. The shore was empty, the

undergrowth seemed impenetrable. Their listening ears caught nothing but the cries of birds and the sultry roar of the waves breaking on the reef outside the lagoon. Neither was there any grass for picnics.

'I think it is a desert island,' said Aunt Hegarty, putting aside her telescope with what seemed like relief. 'We will all sleep on board tonight and go ashore in the morning.'

The nieces were deeply disappointed, but darkness fell suddenly on their grumbles and they went to sleep after a mug of goat's milk apiece and a few sultanas. Emma shared her milk with the cat.

They awoke soon after dawn. For one thing a whole chorus of bird-calls and canticles rose from the island, while pangs of hunger reminded them that the hope of food was only just across the water and they were anxious to be up and away in search of it.

'Very well!' said Aunt Hegarty. 'Lower the lifeboat.'

Since the *Happy-Go-Gay* was as immovable as a trussed duck in the middle of the lagoon, with a sagging sail and no fuel for her boilers, there was nothing to be gained by leaving anyone aboard her, so they packed a little case with the presents, took the pigeon and Captain Bligh and dropped the goat with the rest of them into the lifeboat. They even took their Sunday clothes, hoping to find some fresh water and wash out their weekday cottons.

It seemed very strange to be rowing away from the *Happy-Go-Gay*, leaving her all alone on the lagoon. They really had not realized what she looked like before.

And how strange the sand felt after the hard planks of the deck! Not that it was the kind of sand they were accustomed to at Margate, or at Felixstowe. It was very hard and prickly, being made up, in fact, of thousands of little pieces of broken shell. The goat picked up her feet awkwardly, and none of the nieces felt inclined to take their shoes and stockings off.

But the gorgeous butterfly, or one very like it, had flown

ahead to welcome them to the shore, and was teasing Captain Bligh by taking flights just ahead of the kitten's nose, and remaining just out of reach all the time.

'There *are* coconuts!' said Emma. 'And the palm trees are just *like* palm trees!'

'There's fruit!' said Sophie, pointing to the bushes.

'Eat only a very little at first!' Aunt Hegarty warned them. 'Then, if it does you no harm, you can eat some more.'

In spite of their hunger, they were careful, for nobody wanted to be poisoned the first day on a desert island, so for half an hour or more they walked around asking each other politely if they felt quite well? When it seemed that the fruit was harmless, they all fell to and feasted, and nothing before had ever tasted quite so good.

Rose discovered a little fresh water stream dropping between two rocks into a pool on the shore. With cries of joy they drank their fill, bathed their faces and hands, watered the goat, and were about to begin a general washing of clothes when Aunt Hegarty sternly rallied them to her side.

'There is work to be done first!' she commanded. 'In conditions like these a washing day counts as recreation. Before any of you washes so much as a pocket handkerchief, the hold of the *Happy-Go-Gay* must be filled with coconuts so that we can have fuel, food and drink for our future needs. Not a corner must be left empty. Now you have eaten and drunk your fill there is no time to be lost.'

The nieces were flabbergasted. After all the adventures and strain of the last few days they had counted on a holiday and a rest on this beautiful island. And they were not to be allowed so much as a nap in the sun!

Annie, who might have been expected to be a little more eager than the others to be up and on their way, grumbled loudest of all.

Aunt Hegarty took no notice. She organized a party to collect coconuts and another to form a kind of chain, passing them from hand to hand, down to the lifeboat.

When the boat was full Aunt Hegarty, Lucy and Emma rowed it back to the steamer and undertook the tedious work of transporting all the coconuts into the hold and stocking them as closely as possible.

It was impressive to think that in these horny hairy shells lay all their food and most of their drink perhaps for weeks to come. The husks too would be their only fuel until they came to another island with something more suitable growing on it. Somehow coal did not seem to go with palm trees.

Lucy patted her boilers as though promising them a handsome dinner.

When they rowed back to the shore a fine pile of coconuts was waiting for them and this time Sophie, Emma and Rose did the ferrying.

By then it was time for another meal of fruit, washed down by goat's milk. The goat had been grazing among the undergrowth and had plenty of milk for everybody. Dinner was a feast, and if anyone had a stomach-ache it was not because the fruit was poisonous.

The day passed before they knew it, they had been so busy, but the hold was filled to capacity, and although their limbs ached and their heads throbbed with toiling under the hot sun, they had a sense of pride and achievement that a washing day could never have provided.

'Need we sleep on board? It's so *hot*!' said Annie.

The deck of the *Happy-Go-Gay* was certainly hot. All day long the sun had beaten down on her planking and the rails scorched their hands when they climbed on board. Even when the sun plunged down into the sea, leaving a strange pale light reflecting off the lagoon, the steamer seemed stiflingly hot and the cabin quite airless.

'*Do* let's sleep on the island!' begged the nieces.

Aunt Hegarty hesitated, but finally agreed. Rose and Harriet rowed back to the steamer to fetch mattresses and blankets, in case the dawn were chilly.

They wrapped themselves up like cocoons till the beauty of the tropical night lulled them one by one to sleep. The far night call of birds, the lapping of the waves, and the soft swishing of palm tree branches soothed the pangs of over-active digestion stimulated by a surfeit of fruit and coconuts. Fears that had gathered in the darkness evaporated. Prayers said under the stars gathered them into a closer Protection. Only Aunt

Hegarty sat upright, taking the first two hours of the night watch, till she should waken Emma to take her place.

Out in the lagoon the *Happy-Go-Gay* seemed to keep guard over them all.

So they could hardly believe it when they awoke in the morning and found the goat was gone.

Chapter Fourteen

The Search

The goat had simply vanished.

'She was there in *my* watch! I heard her chewing the cud!' said Emma.

'And I did!' said Harriet.

'She got up when Harriet woke me!' said Sophie. 'And I heard her lie down again and go on chewing.'

'I know she was there in *my* watch!' said Annie.

'How do you know?' asked Lucy fiercely.

Annie went very red.

She had been sitting there fast asleep when Lucy awoke for her watch and found the goat gone.

'She can't be far away! She knows me! She'll come to be milked!' said Emma, but Aunt Hegarty was closely examining the rope that had tied the goat to the palm tree, quite close beside their little camp. Something sharp had cut it right through the strands.

Horror spread among the nieces. To think that someone had been as close to them as that, at some time during the night, and had stolen the goat under their very noses!

'Oh, if we'd only slept on the *Happy-Go-Gay*!' moaned Harriet.

'Or if Annie hadn't gone to sleep!' said Emma.

All the nieces looked accusingly at Annie who looked the other way.

Along the shore the undergrowth was so thick and dense it did not seem possible to lead a full-sized goat through it, but presently they found a narrow track leading back into the bush and in the entrance to the track were the prints of tiny pointed hoofs.

'This way! This way!' cried Emma.

'Wait!' said Aunt Hegarty. 'If the goat has been stolen it means there is someone on the island. If there is someone it might be savages. If there are savages they may be dangerous. We should be extremely foolish to plunge into the interior knowing nothing of the country or its people. For all we know they are just setting a trap for us to walk into.'

'But what can we do?' said Emma. 'How can we just forsake the goat? What will it think of us?'

'Better than being killed!' shivered Harriet, looking backwards into the dark interior and making up her mind that nothing on earth would induce her to penetrate those shadows.

'No more milk!' said Lucy, turning fiercely on Annie. 'It's all your fault!' she snapped.

It was the last thing they remembered saying to Annie. A few minutes later she, like the goat, had completely disappeared.

Nobody saw her go. Certainly nobody came and took her. One minute she was there and the next she just wasn't. They called and shouted in vain.

'It's a disappearing island!' said Emma, bursting into tears. 'How perfectly horrible!'

'I think she's gone to look for the goat because of what you said, Lucy,' said Harriet. 'So it's your fault this time!'

'Well *I'm* not going to disappear!' said Lucy, clinging firmly to Emma. 'If we do it, let's do it all together.'

'Nobody is to disappear again unless they want to be Court Martialled,' said Aunt Hegarty severely. 'We must all keep strictly together. Sophie, you are to be responsible for Emma, Emma for Lucy, Lucy for Harriet and Harriet for Rose. None of you is to go out of my sight for a single moment. And now we are going into the forest immediately to look for Annie and the goat.'

With Aunt Hegarty leading they entered the narrow track that led between the prickly mangroves and bushes into the darkness of the interior. A cool green light enveloped them. They could only walk in Indian file but held one another's hands and kept as closely as possible together. They carried their possessions with them. Their mattresses and blankets had been packed away in the lifeboat, and the boat pushed underneath some roots on the shore, where it was nearly invisible.

Emma carried Captain Bligh and Rose had the remaining pigeon in its cage. Sophie carried the case with the presents in it, which also contained their Sunday velvets.

Aunt Hegarty used her butterfly net as a walking-stick, but had the chopping axe hung from her waistbelt. It was the only weapon of defence they possessed.

They moved very silently, listening for the bleat of a goat, or the sound of Annie's voice. But the cries and screams of hundreds of birds filled the forest, and each cry sounded like the hostile shout of a band of savages.

The track grew broader as they left the shore behind them. Presently they were able to walk two abreast, and it seemed as if people used it quite frequently. The ground was flattened and the creepers were pushed aside.

They hurried along but Annie must have sped like a deer ahead of them. They had almost given up hope of finding her when Sophie picked up her hair ribbon. They were about to shout her name when Aunt Hegarty pointed out the ashes of a camp fire in a little glade close by. The fire was not very new, but neither was it very old.

'There are people somewhere. Hush!' she warned the nieces.

Morning melted into afternoon and everyone was tired and hungry. A few berries snatched from the bushes was all the food they allowed themselves. They seemed to have been walking for ever, and the *Happy-Go-Gay* might have been a thousand miles behind them.

'If only we could find Annie *or* the goat!' sighed Sophie. 'I don't see how we can possibly find both.'

'Unless we find something very soon we shall have to turn back and start again early tomorrow,' said Aunt Hegarty. 'I am not going to risk being overtaken by darkness in this jungle. We must sleep at least on the shore.'

But every turn in the track led them on to another, and every fresh corner seemed more hopeful, so they pressed on in spite of the waning afternoon, and in fact the trees were so dense that the time of day made very little difference to the strange green light of the world inside the jungle.

'After this corner we shall turn about,' said Aunt Hegarty, and when the corner was turned and the track still ran on with no change and giving no clue to its destination, they halted at last and prepared to return all the long weary way back to the shore, empty-handed, hope fading, yet looking back over their shoulders with a last prayer that something would still emerge from the shadows to end their quest.

Nothing emerged, but suddenly Emma said: 'I hear drums!'

Behind them, up the wayward track, half muffled by bird chatter and monkey cries, came the beat of drums, spasmodic, rhythmical, *human* – as if someone were quite patiently calling a large scattered family to come to dinner.

Without a word, but much more cautiously than before, Aunt Hegarty led her little party in the direction of the drum-beats. They moved up the track so quietly that they could hardly hear each other's movements, on and on towards the softly throbbing drums, and it was therefore with the most shattering surprise that someone sprang violently out of the bushes beside them crying 'Stop!'

Chapter Fifteen

In the Native Village

It was Annie. She was hot and dishevelled and her hair fell in wild strands about her face, since she had lost her hair ribbon. Her clothes were torn and ragged and she looked hungry.

'Don't go on!' she warned them in a loud whisper. 'There are lots and lots of them and they've got it!'

'I suppose you mean they have got the goat,' said Aunt Hegarty. 'It was very wrong of you to go after it all by yourself, Annie, and give us such a fright. We have been following you for most of the day.'

'*I* lost it. I had to find it,' said Annie with a rather irritating air of conscious martyrdom. 'And it's there. Only there are thousands of savages too and we'll never get it back alive.'

'How do you know they are *savages*?' said Aunt Hegarty. 'Or that they won't give it back to us? Natives have just as clear an idea of property as anyone. I have treated with dozens of them in my time. Join on behind us and keep close to Rose and we will see what kind of people they are to deal with.'

Leading her little party forward, Aunt Hegarty strode with some dignity up the remaining few yards of the track, which widened suddenly into a circle of native huts, in the centre of which a large number of natives were sitting around their Chief, an extremely handsome old man who was examining their goat with every appearance of admiration and interest.

The goat was held by a small boy, scarcely bigger than Emma, who seemed very proud of himself, although so dusty and footsore that they had little doubt he was responsible for stealing her.

The natives greeted Aunt Hegarty's arrival with great surprise, but showed no fear and certainly no antagonism. Within a moment they had cleared a path to the Chief and led Aunt Hegarty and her nieces to his side.

Aunt Hegarty held out her hand which the old man shook up and down several times very gently.

'Sir, we are English travellers,' Aunt Hegarty began. 'And we greet you in the name of Her Majesty Queen Victoria of England.'

'Yes! Yes!' nodded the Chief, looking pleased. 'Greet her how-do. Very happy to see you. Very thank you for nice goat.'

'Dear sir, we have other presents for you, much better than old she-goat,' said Aunt Hegarty quickly. 'Your boy took away our goat in the night. My nieces were very sad about it. She is a bad old goat, no good at all, but my nieces are very fond of her. She belongs to the family.'

The old Chief nodded, smiling kindly at the nieces who could think so foolishly about a useless goat. 'Give it back!' he ordered the little boy, who did so with the injured air of one who has walked barefoot all day long for nothing.

Aunt Hegarty was beckoning Sophie to come forward with the presents when the Chief interrupted her, waving them aside.

'Presently later,' he said. 'Now you will stay and be my guests. You will eat and drink and rest and my wife will look after you.'

A comfortable hut was put at their disposal and delicious food set before them, also, more welcome still after their exhausting day, water to wash in and cool grass mats to lie on after they had eaten.

The Chief's wife spoke English nearly as well as he did. She too had travelled to England for the coronation of Queen Victoria, and had many questions to ask about London and the Houses of Parliament, the beefeaters in the Tower and the wonderful exhibition of waxworks made by Madame Tussaud.

No one could have made them more welcome, and so relaxed and at home did they feel that Annie was tempted to forget her manners and ask a question that embarrassed them all.

'Do you ever eat people here?' she asked.

The Chief's wife looked scandalized, and then she smiled kindly at Annie as on a child that knows no better, as she gently replied:

'Oh no never, never. Only our enemies.'

When the Chief's wife had left the hut the others set upon Annie and reduced her to tears.

'Orphanage manners!' Rose taunted, and had her ears boxed by Aunt Hegarty.

'I am positive the orphanage would be as ashamed of Annie's

manners as I am of yours,' said Aunt Hegarty, so Rose cried too. It was quite a relief to be safely crying for bad manners when everyone had recently been so anxious and afraid.

They all went to sleep feeling quite relaxed and happy.

In the morning bright sunshine was splashing into the circle of huts, where trees had been cut down to make room for the village. Children and dogs were running about, cocks were crowing and women beating their washing on wet stones beside a watersplash.

Food was brought them, with more water for drinking and washing, after which Aunt Hegarty waited ceremoniously upon the Chief with the presents they had brought.

It was rather an embarrassing occasion.

A Chief who had travelled to England and been on a conducted tour of the Houses of Parliament was not likely to be impressed by trinkets bought in the Penny Bazaar. And they had so little to offer him other than these.

Emma hoped and prayed that they might not, after all, have to give back the goat. There were cats and pigeons in the village already. Nobody had shown the slightest interest in Captain Bligh or Queener Sheba.

But Aunt Hegarty betrayed none of her qualms.

'Chief,' she began, 'these trifles that we bring from England are only worthy, we know, of your women and children. For you we have something better. You have many lovely butterflies in your country, and you must often want to catch them. We have brought you a butterfly net.'

The old Chief accepted Aunt Hegarty's butterfly net with obvious disappointment.

'Can I kill my enemies with this net?' he asked, turning it over and over.

'No, not enemies. It is for catching butterflies,' Aunt Hegarty said reprovingly.

'My butterflies don't hurt me. My enemies do!' said the Chief disconsolately.

Suddenly he caught sight of the axe hanging at Aunt Hegarty's belt and reached forward beaming with pleasure.

'Thank you, very great thank you for beautiful axe! Chop up my enemies *and* my butterflies!' he announced in triumph, and there was no help for it but to unfasten the axe and give it to him. After all, they had already refused him the goat and at the moment the obligations were all on their side.

The Chief did not seem to think so however. He thanked them again most reverently for the splendid weapon and announced that later in the day he would take them for an English picnic and show them his treasures.

'In England we went picnic in a little pony cart!' he told them, laughing. 'But here my people carry you.'

Three beautifully hung litters did in fact arrive into which the nieces packed themselves, three in each, while the Chief and Aunt Hegarty travelled in the largest and most splendid. Inside, the litters were pale and cool like tents, but the swaying movement of the bearers made them all feel sick and they were glad to scramble out some half an hour away from the village, and find themselves on a rocky hillside with the sun pouring down, but a pleasantly cool and puffy breeze rollicking down from the peaks above.

They had paused beside a rock face, and while the bearers and other natives carrying baskets of food flung themselves down on the grassy sward – real grass, if a little scrubby and prickly – the Chief beckoned Aunt Hegarty down a narrow passage between the rocks, that became narrower and darker the farther they penetrated into the mountain.

'I don't like it a bit!' said Harriet as they left the sunshine behind them and walked between damp walls of rock studded with small, spiky plants and bushes. 'Can't we go back and wait for them outside?'

'I want to see his treasure!' said Annie obstinately.

'It is close by now!' came the voice of the old Chief. 'Here is the door!'

It was a doorway rather than a door. At an acute right angle a very narrow opening gave entrance to some cave or corridor that looked so sinister and dark from without that all the nieces stopped dead in their tracks.

'I'm not going in there!' Harriet said, but the old Chief's voice urged them on.

'Follow me! Quite safe!' he assured them, and Aunt Hegarty followed him, stoutly squeezing after him through the crack. Sophie followed, and one by one the others went too.

They found themselves standing in a cave, and high high

above them was a patch of sky, the only light that illuminated the Chief's treasure, piled here in drifts and mounds upon the floor, becoming more vivid and brilliant as every moment their eyes became more and more accustomed to the darkness.

There were emeralds – thousands of emeralds, gleaming like

the eyes of jewelled cats. There were red rubies and blue sapphires, diamonds, pearls, golden rings, topazes, agates, amethysts, aquamarines and a host of precious stones lying on the ground, not like discarded trash, but like doyens of a secret kingdom all their own.

'My treasures!' said the Chief simply. 'My people digged them from the mountains. All for me.'

'They are wonderful beyond words!' said Aunt Hegarty.

The Chief nodded.

'I took five jewels as present to Buckingham Palace with me,' he said. 'Great Queen Victoria was very happy indeed. You are good kind noble people,' the Chief said, facing them. 'I would give you as much as you can carry of my jewels. But for you I have something still better.'

Emma felt Annie's hand, hot and excited, clutching hers in the dark.

'The ransom!' she was whispering in Emma's ears. 'The ransom! Now we shall be able to ransom the boys!'

Emma nodded violently in the dark. It hardly seemed polite to comment aloud in front of the Chief. She would have liked to put her arms round his neck and hug him.

'You are very generous, Chief!' Aunt Hegarty replied. 'You have been kind and magnanimous to us and we shall tell Her Majesty of your courtesy. We do not need presents over and above your hospitality.'

'We do! Oh, we do!' cried Annie in whispered agony. Emma was afraid the Chief would hear her.

'Dear good lady, my pleasure is to give you very, very beautiful present, as beautiful as this!' said the Chief, touching the axe that now swung at his belt.

'Just a pearl or a small jewel to remember you by,' said Aunt Hegarty, but the Chief brushed the jewels pettishly aside with his foot.

'The mountains are full of jewels,' he said. 'My people dig them up, they polish them, they rest here. My treasure. But for you I have something nobody else has, not my friends, not my enemies, something I give to you alone. Wait here!'

He disappeared into a corner of the cave and they heard him searching and seeking. Wrappings rustled as he drew something out of the shadows, and they saw he was unfolding large leaves that swathed some carefully parcelled object. Something gleamed in the dark. The nieces trembled with excitement and Annie's fingers curled so tightly round Emma's arm that it was all she could do not to scream and say 'Don't!'

Even Sophie believed that the object in the Chief's hands

must be a casket full of golden pieces, or precious stones, but only Annie cried aloud with the sharpness of her disappointment when the object proved to be a gilt Coronation mug with a portrait of Queen Victoria engraved upon it.

Fortunately the Chief took her cry for admiration. He held the mug where it would best catch the light, and then pressed it into Aunt Hegarty's hands with deep pride, and a touchingly dignified gesture of renunciation.

Aunt Hegarty's thanks were also ceremonious and dignified. The nieces dutifully added their gratitude. Only Annie's mouth remained obstinately shut and she looked the other way.

Pleased with their reception of his present, the Chief led the way out of the cave, and one by one Aunt Hegarty and the nieces followed him.

The mug was acclaimed with cries of admiration by the natives waiting outside the cave. They showed by their nods and smiles how suitable a present they considered it to be for their honoured visitors.

The picnic was already spread, and the moment the Chief was seated fruit and meats were handed round. Everyone was hungry except Annie, who sat brooding, picking at her food and refusing to speak to anybody.

'It's no good grieving over it!' Emma tried to console her, 'Aunt Hegarty had promised to arrange about a ransom the moment we get home and you'll soon have your brothers back again!'

Annie merely shrugged her shoulders and would not answer. Emma left her alone.

They travelled back to the village at a leisurely pace and were glad to fling themselves on the grass mats inside the hut and rest. Food was brought them later in the evening and they all retired to bed.

Aunt Hegarty had noticed Annie's sullen face and guessed the reason.

'My dear child, you are fretting because the Chief did not let us help ourselves to his treasures,' she said. 'Don't you realize that he has given us kindness, which is worth more than all his jewels put together – besides the greatest treasure that he has, in his own eyes?' and she touched the Coronation mug.

'*That* won't ransom the boys!' said Annie violently.

'I can understand your anxiety,' Aunt Hegarty said, ignoring her rudeness. 'But I think I can set your mind at rest. In the

morning I am going to see the Chief alone and tell him the whole story. Then I shall ask him frankly for just enough jewels to make a good ransom, no more and no less, and I have no doubt whatever that he will give them to us. He is a generous man as you can see and I believe he will do all he can to help his friends. I can always arrange for it to be a loan.'

The nieces looked at Annie to watch her relief, but to their great surprise instead of smiling for joy she leapt to her feet, and stamping on the mud-caked floor of the hut she shouted:

'There isn't any need to! I've got it already!' and out of her pocket streamed a flow of brilliant jewels, pouring on to the floor.

Chapter Sixteen

Restitution

There was a stunned silence.

Sophie said afterwards that she felt perfectly sick from the shock, and everybody else felt the same. Aunt Hegarty turned rather pale and drew herself up so tall and straight that she seemed to tower like a great eagle over the unfortunate Annie, now sobbing in a sudden agony of shame and remorse.

'*Annie!*' said Aunt Hegarty in a terrible ice-cold voice. 'I'm absolutely ashamed and mortified to think that you are a niece of mine. Never, *never* would I have given you a berth upon the *Happy-Go-Gay* if I had dreamed you capable of such baseness!'

Annie fell to her knees, sobbing for pardon. 'It was the ransom for the boys!' she wept.

'And do you think for one moment that Charleyboy and Gustus, who from almost first to last have behaved like English gentlemen – do you think they would have *accepted* to be ransomed by such low and contemptible means as this!' said Aunt Hegarty.

'I'll give it back! I'll give it back!' sobbed Annie.

'That is the very least you can do!' said Aunt Hegarty. 'But how can you ever undo the harm you have done? How can you mend the hurt to this fine old man who has done everything in his power to make us comfortable and happy in his village? What will he think when he realizes his most precious gift of all was not enough and, not content with it, that we have stolen – *stolen* – his jewels as well?'

All the nieces were now in tears, but fortunately the goat began to bleat so loudly in sympathy that nobody outside the hut was likely to notice their distress.

'She wasn't really as greedy as all that, Aunt Hegarty! She only did it for Charleyboy and Gustus!' sniffed Emma.

'Two wrongs don't make a right, Emma,' said Aunt Hegarty coldly.

Annie began feverishly to collect the jewels from the floor. One by one she stuffed them back into her pockets, hiccoughing and sobbing the while.

'I'm going to take them back now!' she said. 'I'm going there by myself to put them back in the cave. Then he'll never know and his feelings won't be hurt and he'll still like us.'

Aunt Hegarty nodded almost approvingly.

'I really think that is the best thing to do,' she said. 'There are times when a little deception softens a grievous blow. But I cannot allow you to go alone, Annie. I am the leader of this expedition and you are still under my orders. The forest is strange and full of dangers, you cannot be unprotected. We must all go together.'

The other nieces suppressed a groan of dismay. Annie looked very cross. Emma could see she had hoped to play a kind of heroine's part.

'They keep no watch, I noticed that last night,' said Aunt Hegarty. 'It is not so very far, and we shall be back before dawn. Everybody in the village seems to be asleep. I will make sure that no one is stirring, and then we will start.'

'What about the animals?' said Emma anxiously. 'The goat won't stop bleating all night if we leave her alone and they may come in and find we are gone. And Captain Bligh cries terribly when I'm not there. I'm not sure about the pigeon either.'

'We had better take them with us,' said Aunt Hegarty.

They stole out of the hut and plunged into the forest, making a wide circuit in single file until they met the track they had travelled in the morning.

Nobody wanted to talk. Aunt Hegarty walked first, with Annie. Emma and the goat brought up the rear. Even the goat seemed too subdued to bleat, and besides, Emma was holding her very tightly by the collar.

There was no difficulty in finding their way. The track was lit by a magnificent tropical moon, nearly at its full, and but for the eeriness of the light, it might have been daytime. The shadows however were deep and strange, unknown birds gibbered, unexpected branches creaked, soft jungle feet padded in every direction, and the background stillness of the night seemed loudest of all.

Rose got a thorn in her foot, and in removing it Emma let Captain Bligh go, and moonstruck, he ran up a tree. It took over half an hour to get him down. Emma would not leave him crying there, pretending he was frightened and clinging to the trunk with agonized claws, yet when at last they dragged her away sobbing he was after them before they had rounded a second corner. Rose slapped him so hard he bit her.

At last they came out on the hillside and their spirits rose. There was the flattened picnic patch, there was the cleft in the rocks, darker and more menacing than ever it had seemed by daylight. There was the sparkling stream where they had drunk at the picnic, and one and all ran to drink again, as if the cold, happy, tumbling water made them feel braver.

Lucy even splashed Emma a little, and they were drying their hands on their cloaks when Aunt Hegarty said: 'Quiet!'

Everyone froze on the spot. At first there was nothing to be heard, and then suddenly there was something. Voices below, low and spasmodic, coming up the patch behind them!

Quickly they glanced around them but the mountainside offered no shelter and the forest was far below them. They would be visible as far above as the peaks themselves, and their only hope was to hide in the cave and hope there were some recesses beyond in which they could crouch, should anyone come searching.

But the passage was narrow, the goat was stubborn, and it took quite a little while for all the nieces, the goat and finally Aunt Hegarty to slide through the cleft and then round the corner into the cave.

'Stand against the wall!' Aunt Hegarty murmured. 'Try to be flat. Put the goat behind you, Emma! Muffle Captain Bligh. And now – absolute quiet!'

They could only hope and pray that whoever was coming up the path would pass by the passage in the rock, or, if they did come in, would simply look round the doorway into a cave without entering.

So they stood without breathing for what seemed hours and hours while the voices grew louder outside, and then louder still, and at last could only be entering the corridor.

There was a terrible silence and then . . .

Emma's heartbeats sounded to her like the thunder of drums when she realized that the old Chief and some of his followers were actually looking past them, right into the cave, and that at any moment they might distinguish Aunt Hegarty and her nieces from among the shadows that were now their only disguise.

They recognized the Chief's voice, but they could no longer understand what he said, since he was speaking in his own language, but his tone was excitable, agitated, and angry.

Tense and breathless they waited for him to step into the cave, but he only peered from the doorway, querying, questioning, debating with his companions.

Fear paralysed them till nobody *could* have coughed or sneezed. Even breathing was almost beyond them. Yet out of the absolute stillness came a sudden abysmal gulp as the goat began suddenly to chew the cud. Out of the darkness her jaws moved with the sound of tearing paper, and they knew they were discovered.

The anger blazing in the old Chief's eyes transformed him from the gentle host they had known into a vision of fury. And his fury became little short of frenzy when he saw Annie furtively trying to empty her pockets of jewels, just a few minutes too late – if anything could have made things worse at this juncture.

In vain she flung herself at his feet and attempted to explain: he would not listen to a word from any of them.

Five minutes later, their hands tied behind their backs with trailing creepers, they were being marched back down the track towards the village. The goat followed, bleating miserably. One of the bodyguard carried the pigeon. Captain Bligh had to walk.

Chapter Seventeen

Prisoners in the Pit

Early dawn was breaking when the prisoners, one after another, were dropped into a square pit on the edge of the circle of huts, partly sheltered by palm trees, but very hot and stuffy at the bottom.

The animals were thrown in too, the pigeon in the cage being flung down last of all. Captain Bligh was the only one who landed without a shaking.

It was not difficult to see what had happened. The hut next to theirs must have accidentally caught fire during the night for it was now a heap of ashes. In going to rouse their guests the villagers had discovered that Aunt Hegarty and her party had disappeared. Searchers had been dispatched in all directions, and the old Chief's party had been the one to bring them home.

All the villagers came to look at them during the morning and jabber their disapproval. They were no longer honoured guests but objects of contempt and scorn.

Presently their attitude changed. Instead of scolding and shouting they began to jump about the edge of the pit looking hopeful and rubbing their stomachs.

'She said they ate their enemies! We're all enemies now!' Annie said, bursting into tears for the twentieth time. The rest said nothing. They were plunged into such utter doom and depression that there did not seem anything left to say.

'I don't expect they'll eat the goat or Captain Bligh,' Emma said, fondling her pets. 'And we might as well let Queener

Sheba go. She's the only one of us who *can* get away if she wants to.'

'I think we ought to send a message to dear Mamma and dear Papa,' said Sophie stifling a sob. 'Just tell them what is happening to us. They'd want to know.'

'Not about being eaten,' gulped Harriet. 'Just say "Put To Death by Cannibals".'

'Ask them to tell Matron,' said Annie. 'Oh! Oh! Now Charleyboy and Gustus will never be ransomed!'

'I think it would be much more sensible to simply ask Mr Mumpus to send help,' said Aunt Hegarty. 'After all, we don't *know* we are going to be eaten, and if we are there is no time to be lost.'

Rose wrote out a message of appeal as quickly as she was able, and added their address, as far as they were able to give it.

By now the people of the village had grown tired of staring down at them, and they were able to set Queener Sheba free with the message tied under her wing, and loose her from the pit without causing any excitement. Everyone had a drink of goat's milk and for a short while everyone felt better.

The long day passed away. Towards evening, one of the Chief's servants dropped some fruit into the pit, but at the same time they saw natives carrying large bundles of brushwood, which hinted horribly at preparations for cooking-fires and other necessities for making stews.

As darkness fell they sat trembling and waiting in the pit, expecting at any moment to be fished out to meet their fate, but although there was considerable activity in the village above, nobody came near them.

'I expect they're waiting for full moon,' said Annie firmly. 'It's the day after tomorrow. Look, there's still a little bit to grow!'

The moon was shining down into the pit, as brightly as it had lighted their way to the treasure cave the night before, but it was still not completely round. The night was cool and they were glad to wrap themselves in their cloaks and tie their sun-bonnets closely underneath their chins. Even so, it was difficult to sleep.

'Can't you keep still?' Sophie asked Annie crossly. Annie kept fidgeting and kicking at the side of the pit.

'I can't sleep, and I can't just do *nothing*!' said Annie with more spirit than she had shown since their capture. 'Besides there's a funny bit here. It sounds hollow!'

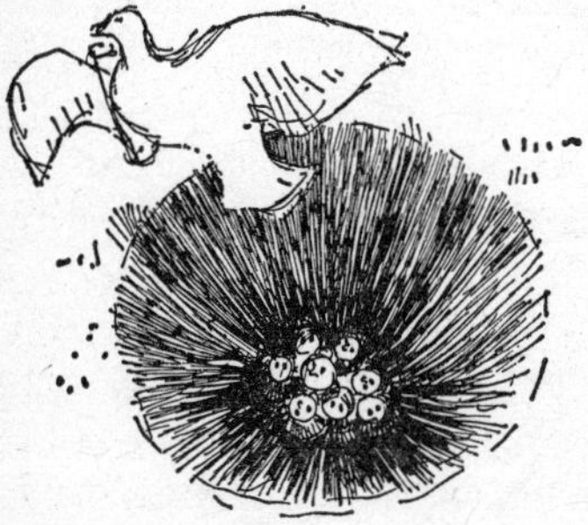

'*Hollow?*' said Sophie. Annie just went on scratching and kicking. She was still scratching and kicking when the sun rose in the morning, but the pitside seemed no more hollow than it had done before, though Annie's nails were broken and she had nearly worn through the toe-caps of her boots.

Nobody came near them all next day. The Chief sent them no more fruit. If they had not had goat's milk to drink they would have suffered terribly from thirst.

Suddenly, in the middle of the afternoon there was a cry of triumph from Annie.

'There! I knew it was hollow and it is!' she cried.

They had long ceased to take any notice of Annie's scratching and fidgeting. Now they became aware that she had with her bare hands scratched away a large hollow in one corner of the pit, and that all of a sudden she was able to plunge her arm into it right up to the shoulder.

Aunt Hegarty and the nieces crowded round her. One after another they plunged their arms in too and found a void beyond the earth and stones that Annie was rapidly scraping out of the way.

'It's an underground passage!' said Lucy.

'It's just another pit!' said Rose, but it was not.

First Annie was able to put her legs inside. Then she crept

in on all fours and disappeared altogether. Finally she came out backwards with her face all covered with earth and announced in triumph:

'It *is* a passage! And it goes on and on. I can't even see the other end of it!'

'We can *escape*!' cried the nieces, prepared one and all to dive into the underground tunnel after Annie and to go wherever it might lead them.

'Wait!' said Aunt Hegarty. 'If we go now the very first villager who passes by and looks over the edge will raise the alarm and they will come after us and catch us. We must wait until they have all gone to bed.'

'But suppose they mean to eat us tonight!' said Sophie.

'There is that danger,' Aunt Hegarty agreed. 'But they will light the fires quite early if they do.'

'To get the water hot,' said Annie glumly.

'They have not lit them yet,' said Aunt Hegarty. 'If they do we must go at once and take our chance before they come to fetch us. But I feel almost certain that they will wait for full moon. We shall soon know.'

They waited listening, their hearts beating fast and the moments dragging, but as darkness fell there were still no signs of the fires being lit.

'Not tonight!' said Lucy in relief.

'Then we've wasted two whole hours!' said Annie, who could hardly wait to put her escape route into use.

But she had hardly spoken before a shower of bananas and other fruits were thrown down from above.

'There they are! Aunt Hegarty was right!' said Emma. 'They'd have discovered it at once if we'd gone into the tunnel and they had found us gone.'

'They won't eat us now if they bother to give us supper,' Sophie said. 'I think it is rather nice of them really.'

'They certainly won't trouble us any more tonight,' Aunt Hegarty said. 'We must make our preparations and get away as quickly as possible.'

She wrote a little letter to the Chief, explaining as best she could just what had happened, and enclosing their deepest apologies. This she put inside the Coronation mug which had never left their hands, but which was now carefully wrapped in leaves and placed in a corner of the pit.

Aunt Hegarty now arranged the nieces' cloaks and sunbonnets to resemble as closely as possible six or seven sleeping figures, just in case anyone peeped down on them during the night.

'It is eight o'clock,' said Aunt Hegarty looking at her watch. 'By eight tomorrow we should be back on the *Happy-Go-Gay*. Into the tunnel now. Annie, you lead. I shall come last.'

Chapter Eighteen

The Escape

To fumble blindly into an unknown underground passage, without the vaguest idea where it will come out, is an ordeal few people would choose to experience, except to save their lives.

There was even the awful possibility that it might emerge in the Chief's hut, or at any rate within full sight and earshot of the village.

So the longer it continued the more hopeful they became, and although the discomfort of groping in the dark, with the constant smell of damp earth and very little air, was almost more than they could endure, the terror of what lay behind them urged them on, and every yard brought more hope of eventual safety.

Suddenly Annie at the front called back: 'I see moonlight!' The word passed back from niece to niece and finally to Aunt Hegarty, 'Annie sees moonlight!' by which time Annie had actually come to the end of the tunnel and was scrambling out into the moonlit forest, gazing around her as if the shadowy jungle were the loveliest thing she had ever seen in all her life, as indeed at that moment she felt it was.

One after the other they emerged, shaking the earth out of their hair. Emma hugged Captain Bligh and the goat in turn in her delight.

They were quite a long way from the village. That is to say they could hear no voices and see no light.

'Come along!' said Aunt Hegarty. 'We don't want the goat to

start bleating and betray us. We can find our way by the moon and the stars. Follow me.'

It was not so simple as all that. True the passage had emerged into a clearer part of the jungle where at first they could move with ease, but after half a mile or so the undergrowth closed in, till the walls of tall bushes, shrubs and

tangled creepers were nearly as impenetrable as the walls of the pit and they wandered hither and thither trying to press their way through, always to be rebuffed by the dense foliage and stems of the bushes. The thought that they were only a short distance from the village made them desperate, and at last Annie, scratched and bleeding, forced her way through a thicket fierce with thorns and landed quite suddenly on a track leading southward.

The others struggled after her. To make up for lost time they fairly ran down the narrow path till everyone was out of breath, but they felt safe enough to slacken their pace and even to chat a little, for the first time for several hours.

'Do you think the Chief didn't know about the underground passage, Aunt Hegarty?' Rose asked.

'I don't think he expected us to find it,' said Aunt Hegarty. 'Probably some other prisoners made it, a long time ago, and the entrance was filled in afterwards. It took Annie quite a long time to get through, you remember.'

Sophie had bound up Annie's raw fingers with her handkerchief torn into strips. Annie hid them humbly behind her back while Aunt Hegarty was speaking.

'Is this *our* path? The one we came along?' Lucy asked.

'I don't recognize it,' Aunt Hegarty said, and nobody else did either, but naturally it all looked different by moonlight.

'We are going in the right direction,' said Aunt Hegarty. 'When the moon goes down it will be a little more difficult to find our way but there are always the stars to follow.'

'And there is always the track to follow!' sang Annie happily, leading the party so fast that they could scarcely catch up with her. Annie's boots were worn through and she was limping worse than anybody so no one had the face to ask her to go more slowly.

Until all of a sudden the path came to an end, just like that.

It petered out in a little glade, where there were the remains of a fire, and a tumbledown hut, as if hunters had used the place for a kind of hunting lodge. A hut, a glade, a fireplace and some ashes – but no more track.

'Everybody hold hands and keep close behind me,' Aunt Hegarty said. 'This time I shall lead.'

The same old struggle began – the forcing through the bushes, the scratching with thorns. They could only tell they were going in the right direction because of the moon, and slowly, slowly the moon went down.

'Never mind, I know the stars!' said Aunt Hegarty, and she followed the bright pointers sailing over the trees far, far above their heads. Then clouds came up and it began to rain.

They had left their cloaks at the bottom of the pit in the native village. Their sunbonnets were there too, while their Sunday velvets lay packed in the case inside the hut.

The rain soaked their cotton frocks and poured off their unprotected heads on to their shoulders. It dropped from Aunt

Hegarty's hat and reduced Captain Bligh to a pitiful bundle of misery.

Every star was blotted out by the rain. They were in the middle of a forest, with no track, hardly able to see each other for darkness and quite ignorant of their compass directions.

'It's this way!' Annie urged. 'I know it's this way!'

The undergrowth was, in fact, a little less dense in that direction, so Aunt Hegarty allowed her to lead, and when some while later she stumbled on a new track everyone at first thought her very clever.

But the track seemed to lead here there and everywhere (it was, in fact, an old track made by the villagers on their hunting expeditions), and as the rain and the darkness persisted they were soon bewildered and could only hope that at some time it would come out on the shore beside the sea.

They did not realize that they had actually walked in one enormous circle, until the sun rose and they stumbled, almost too weary to realize it, on to the track that led them straight into the native village.

Chapter Nineteen

Back to the Village

Their flight had been discovered. That was the first thing they realized. The village was teeming with activity, and before they had time to turn and flee a dozen natives saw them and came running towards them gesticulating and shouting in excitement.

The next thing they saw was the very large pile of brushwood built up in the very centre of the village, over which large cooking pots had been suspended on thick green branches.

Closing in about them, the villagers led Aunt Hegarty and her nieces down the track in a triumphal procession. The news flew ahead of them and every man, woman and child ran to see them arrive, leaping and waving in the light of the rising sun that began to dapple the huts with patterns of silver and gold. The rain had stopped at last.

The party was marched straight to the hut of the old Chief, who emerged suddenly with his wife beside him, blinking at the early light and quite obviously surprised and delighted at the cause of his early awakening.

To their great astonishment the Chief then came forward, and seizing Aunt Hegarty by the hand began to shake it gently up and down as on their first introduction, while tears filled his eyes and trickled slowly down his cheeks.

'You come back, dear good lady!' he said, shaking his head from side to side. 'You come back to me again!'

Aunt Hegarty did not know what to make of this unexpected reception, and as the rest of the villagers became very silent she and the Chief continued to look at each other, and to shake each other's hands for quite a considerable time.

Then the old man turned and took something from his wife. It was the Coronation mug and out of the mug peeped Aunt Hegarty's letter.

'I understand all things now,' said the Chief. 'I understand. My dear good friends are not thieves and robbers.' Then he pointed at Annie. 'You very, very naughty girl,' he said fiercely. 'When you get back to England your great Queen Victoria eat you up!' but he laughed to show that he was only joking, and added to Aunt Hegarty, 'Very naughty, very *little* girl!'

Annie flushed very red, but she dropped a curtsey and said humbly:

'I am very sorry indeed and I will never do it again!'

When they were escorted back to their original quarters the coolness of their hut and the softness of their grass mats were the most delicious things they could think of at the moment. They slept away the rest of the day with occasional meals of fruit and draughts of cold water brought them by friendly hands.

Their cloaks and sunbonnets were restored to them from the pit, washed, brushed and cleaned. Nobody wanted to have another look into the horrid place, and the Chief and his people did all they could to make them forget about it.

In the evening there was a feast, cooked indeed on the cooking pots over the enormous fires, but composed of deer's meat and every kind of tasty vegetable, after which the mug was once more presented to Aunt Hegarty with great ceremony, for the Chief was quite determined that she should keep it for her own.

When she mentioned that they should be returning now to the *Happy-Go-Gay*, he protested that they could not possibly walk all that distance, but that they should travel in the litters to the shore in the morning.

It was with great thankfulness that they lay down to sleep that night for the last time in the native camp.

After elaborate farewells to the Chief and his wife, Aunt Hegarty's party left in three litters for the shore, the next morning.

The goat was led by the same little boy who had first stolen it away. The nieces found he had become quite a hero in his own village since the villagers were afraid to appear on the shore and preferred to keep to the forests. Apparently the other Paradox Islands held much fiercer and more bloodthirsty tribes, who came in war canoes to wreak havoc on the Chief and his people if they showed their faces.

'I hope they have not attacked the *Happy-Go-Gay*!' said Aunt Hegarty, but the Chief assured her that at the moment the hostile islanders were waging war in another direction.

All the same, he said it would be wiser for his people to set them down at a short distance from the shore and return home in daylight. Aunt Hegarty wholeheartedly agreed.

They slept during most of the journey, making up for the fatigue and danger of their previous adventures.

When at last the trees thinned out and a brightness ahead hinted of the open sea, the men carrying the litters put them down, making their polite farewells, and turned swiftly to begin the long journey home. Sophie was glad to notice they were all wearing treasures from the box they had brought with them, and it was a relief to think that the litters were now empty and perhaps they would take it in turns to give each other rides in them, going home.

It was delightful suddenly to come through the trees on to the sunbaked shore, to paddle at the edge of the lagoon and slap warm salt water on their faces, and above all to see the dear *Happy-Go-Gay* riding at anchor out there on the water, just as they had left her, was it only a few days ago?

The lifeboat too was safely lying in its hiding place, the blanket bags only mildly attacked by crabs or insects.

Cheering with excitement they hauled it down to the shore and piled inside. Then, with Aunt Hegarty, Sophie, Emma and Annie at the oars, they left the desert island and rowed across the water singing, while in the forest the birds went on calling their strange cries and the tropical butterflies fluttered from bush to bush with no one left to admire them.

Chapter Twenty

On Board the 'Happy-Go-Gay'

Aunt Hegarty and her nieces were all as anxious as one another to leave the lagoon and the desert island behind them. Their united, unspoken wish was to start for home.

There were still some hours of daylight left and good little Lucy had already laid the fire inside the boiler. They had brought on board a certain quantity of fruit and filled the life-boat casks with drinking water.

'Start the engines and up anchor!' said Aunt Hegarty.

The first thin whisker of smoke that came out of the stack was greeted with cheers by the rest of the crew, but it was shortly followed by Lucy's anxious face at the hatchway.

'Please Aunt Hegarty, the coconuts won't go into the stoke-hole!'

'Chop them up!' said Aunt Hegarty at once.

And then everybody remembered at the same time that their axe was hanging round the waist of the native Chief.

They tried kitchen knives with no success at all. The hard outer husks resisted as if they had been made out of cast iron. Sophie sacrificed her precious cutting-out scissors, and broke a blade.

Finally Lucy discovered a very small saw down in the hold.

'It is better than nothing,' said Aunt Hegarty. 'We had better saw up a quantity of coconuts and then get up steam and start away.'

Meanwhile the boiler had gone out for lack of priming and

Lucy had to begin all over again. The coconuts took a very long time to saw in pieces. Everyone took turns and soon everyone had blisters. Darkness was falling and as yet there was not enough fuel to take the ferry steamer out of the lagoon. They did not want to drift up against another of the Paradox Islands in the dark.

'I feel I just couldn't stand any more cannibals at present,' Harriet said, sawing for dear life.

The coconuts had to be divided first in one half and then in another before Lucy could push them through the stoke hole.

Meanwhile Aunt Hegarty kept her telescope trained on the horizon in all directions, occasionally sweeping it down the shore of the island behind them. But it would have been a comfort to have seen the kindly face of the native Chief at present.

As darkness fell, Aunt Hegarty gave orders for the sawing to stop. There was a considerable pile of coconut fuel prepared, but not enough to leave the shelter of the lagoon with safety. It was a cloudy night and the moon was obscured.

'We will stop here for the night,' Aunt Hegarty said. 'And in the morning we will up anchor and start for home.'

Disconsolately most of the crew went to bed. Two took the first watch. Aunt Hegarty considered it was safer to watch in pairs at present.

The night passed without incident.

At early dawn Annie was on deck sawing. Taking her watch into consideration she had only had four hours' sleep. 'I'll make it up later,' was all she said.

At seven Aunt Hegarty gave orders to light the boilers. Lucy flew to her post. Once more a puff of smoke crept into the sky and slowly, slowly they began to get up steam.

The coconuts that took so long to quarter burnt up at an alarming rate. Almost half the supplies had already been consumed when the steam gauge rose at last to boiling point and the little whistle on the smokestack began to shrill.

'Up anchor!' cried Aunt Hegarty.

Harriet and Emma hauled on the anchor.

To the cheers of her crew the *Happy-Go-Gay* was on her way at last. Slowly she responded to Aunt Hegarty's hand on the wheel and her bows swung about till they faced the open sea. Slowly her paddle began to slap the water of the lagoon and slowly she paddled forward through the gap in the reef, till the clear, colourful panorama of rock and seaweed under the keel had changed to an opaque blue, churned into a million dancing bubbles by the busy paddles taking up a rhythm that began to sing more and more convincingly, 'We're going home! We're going home! We're going home!'

'Have you got plenty more fuel?' Lucy asked, popping her head out of the engine-room. 'I'm using it up very fast.'

Sophie was sawing.

'Well don't!' she said. 'Try to last it out! I'm sawing as fast as I can!'

'I'll do my best,' Lucy said obligingly. 'But the Admiral says we've got to get full steam ahead till we are clear of the Islands. Isn't she going well? You'd never think those engines had been doing nothing for nearly a week.' She disappeared to feed them.

Although they handed over frequently to each other nobody could saw any faster with such a small, blunt saw, and Lucy's pile of fuel dwindled. Emma was almost ashamed every time she came to fetch more supplies for the engine-room. Because for every four pieces of coconut the workers sawed, Lucy had to put five into the boiler, and sometimes six.

'Lucy, have you *got* to be so extravagant?' Harriet asked.

'Well, you don't want the boiler to go out, do you?' asked Lucy crossly. 'Until Aunt Hegarty tells me to slacken off steam I've simply got to go on stoking. You have no idea how quickly that stuff burns up!'

'Never mind Lucy, we'll keep up with you!' said Annie taking the saw from Harriet, although she had only just finished her turn, and the coconut quarters flew.

'We shall have to saw all night!' Rose whispered, horrified.

The island fell away and became something remote and strange to them, a blue outline that seemed to have no history, nor be any part of the last few days' adventure. The wake connecting them with the lagoon fell away and was blotted out behind them.

'You can take a spell at the wheel, Sophie,' said Aunt Hegarty. 'And it's all right, Lucy, you can go down to half-steam now.'

With the island out of sight and the engines gently throbbing at half-steam, the crew relaxed at last. Some sat down on the deck to bask in the sun, others trotted into the galley to prepare a meal. Captain Bligh began a gigantic toilet and Emma milked the goat. Annie went on sawing coconuts.

Sophie was making a pot of tea.

'I love the sea, don't you?' Emma said to her, filling the milk jug. 'If I had to choose between the devil and the deep blue sea I'd never choose the devil, would you?'

'It's unladylike to talk about the devil. It's unlucky too,' said Sophie, carrying a cup of tea carefully across the deck. 'And what is more, it is very unlucky indeed, because there, if I'm not mistaken, is the devil himself!' And she pointed to the horizon ahead of them, where, bearing down upon them, with all its top gallants set, was the pirate ship.

Chapter Twenty-one

Homeward Bound

Annie might be forgiven if at that moment she wished with all her heart that she still had the native Chief's stolen treasure in her pocket. Dropping the saw, she ran to the rails and stood with her mouth open, gazing at the ship with such an expression of mixed longing and horror that it was almost funny.

Lucy began to stoke for dear life while Emma swung the ship about and called for Aunt Hegarty, who was taking a nap in the sun after two hours at the wheel.

Sophie dropped the teacup and seized the saw, but in her frantic haste she bent the blade which snapped in half.

'Fuel! Lots of Fuel!' Lucy shouted, but the situation was hopeless. Even had the saw not broken, it just was not possible to keep the boiler supplied at full steam, and when Lucy learned the truth, she dropped such tears on the remaining fuel that the coconuts sizzled.

'We can at least meet them with dignity,' said Aunt Hegarty, once more turning the ship about to face the brigantine. 'This time we can hardly expect to buy your freedom. We must say our prayers and hope for some miracle to deliver us.'

She did not even raise her telescope, but steered deliberately for the pirate ship, standing very straight and tall behind the wheel, with a look on her face that made every niece feel herself at once ten times taller and braver.

'Shall we ram her, Aunt Admiral?' said Lucy. 'I believe I have just enough fuel left.'

'Splendid Lucy, splendid!' cried Aunt Hegarty, with what was almost a cheer. 'Better than walking the plank, isn't it, girls? Do you want to fall alive into the pirates' hands?'

'No! No!' shouted the nieces.

'Not really!' said Annie reluctantly, making up her mind to swim round the brigantine till Charleyboy and Gustus pulled her out.

'Then stoke, Lucy! Stoke!' cried Aunt Hegarty, pointing the bows of the *Happy-Go-Gay* right in the middle of the on-coming ship.

Annie's fingers twisted and writhed inside one another. She was peering with all her might at the approaching decks, hoping for the first sight of her brothers. Finally, seeing that Aunt Hegarty was preoccupied, she seized the telescope and put it to her eye.

The whole crew was startled by her cry of excitement.

'There's Charleyboy! And there's Gustus! And there's lots of other boys!'

'Pirates you mean!' said Harriet.

'No *boys* – like Charleyboy and Gustus!' cried Annie. 'They're waving and waving! Charleyboy and Gustus are waving too!'

Harriet snatched the telescope out of her hands.

'It's our brothers!' she shrieked. 'It's Henry! and Edmund! and Benjamin and James! It is! It is!'

'What? Have the pirates got them as well?' said Sophie, horrified.

'There aren't any pirates!' cried Harriet, resisting all efforts to take the telescope away from her. 'There's only boys and they're on the Captain's bridge and running all over the ship. And it isn't the Jolly Roger up there on top any more – it's the Union Jack!'

They had to believe her. At last everyone had a turn with the telescope to see for themselves.

Lucy was called on deck and steam reduced immediately.

Aunt Hegarty put the wheel hard over to avoid a collision and both ships came alongside each other and hove to, the *Happy-Go-Gay* spluttering and sighing over her very last ration of coconut.

'Ahoy there!' came a ringing cheer across the water.

'That's Edmund!' said Sophie.

'Ahoy!' shouted back the crew of the *Happy-Go-Gay*.

'May we come aboard your ship, Adm'ral Ma'am?' came the cry.

'Come aboard and welcome!' cried Aunt Hegarty.

The jollyboat was lowered and once more oars splashed in the sun. Up the ladder scrambled Edmund and Charleyboy, closely followed by Henry and Gustus.

Edmund and his brother kissed Aunt Hegarty's hand and then embraced their sisters.

Annie flung her arms round her brothers' necks but they did not seem to welcome her hugs and kisses.

'Where are the pirates, Edmund?' Sophie asked.

'In the hold, in irons!' Edmund said promptly. 'And there they'll stay until we hand them over to Her Majesty's officers.'

'Poor things!' said Emma, thinking of the pit where they themselves had lain two days as prisoners, even without chains.

'Sister, we feed them like fighting cocks!' said Henry, giving her a smacking kiss. 'All the porridge that Gustus burnt, all the cabbage that didn't last the voyage, all the dish water . . .'

'How cruel!' said Emma, but Edmund patted her shoulder.

'Don't you remember Henry's teasing?' he said kindly. 'No ship under my command is cruel to its prisoners. They do well enough, I promise you. It's a pity Gustus cooks so badly, but he's learning.'

'Yes, I'm learning!' said Gustus cheerfully. He was swelling with pride at serving under the command of such fine fellows as Edmund and Henry.

'But how – *how* did you capture the ship?' Sophie asked.

'Ah!' said Edmund. 'That's another story! When your carrier pigeon arrived home Mr Mumpus sent us the news directly, by telegraph, very smart he was about it too! Unfortunately, or fortunately as the case may be, Papa had taken dear Mamma to Cheltenham for the waters, and we saw there was no time to be

lost, so we hurried to Plymouth and collected the yacht Papa gave Henry and me and set sail.

'Well, we hadn't been a whole day out when we were overhauled by those ruffians who rammed our boat and had us all in the water. They had us swimming about for a while but then they got us on board and shut us down below. We had no idea they had these little fellows aboard as well, not till that night when Charleyboy pinched the key out of the Captain's cabin and let us out. After that it was easy. All the pirates were drunk, or asleep, we only had to pinch some cutlasses and take them prisoner. The Captain was easiest of all. He didn't really wake up till we'd bundled him into the hold. Tut-tut there was a to-do then! We hardly slept a wink all night!'

'Such swearing and cussing!' said Charleyboy, smacking his lips.

'Don't mention the subject in front of ladies and forget anything you have heard!' said Edmund promptly.

'Ay! Ay! Captain!' said Charleyboy, saluting.

'And now if you will honour us by stepping aboard, Ma'am, we have cold meats and wine and some very tolerable dates and raisins,' said Edmund. 'We should be glad to welcome you to dinner.'

'If you give me half an hour I will cook it!' said Sophie.

The crew of the *Happy-Go-Gay* received a royal welcome on board the pirate ship. The boys were anxious to supply them with everything they needed or lacked, from the stores in the brigantine's hold, and soon the nieces were decked out in finely embroidered shawls and scarves that quite transformed their shabby cotton dresses.

Aunt Hegarty still had a prejudice against spoiling velvets by wearing them on shipboard.

The boys listened open-mouthed to their adventures before which the capture of the pirate ship paled to nothing.

'Were the pots really ready to boil?' they asked. 'Were there millions of jewels? Was it a *desert* island? And a real typhoon? How long were you in the pit? And how big was the underground passage?' There was no end to their questions, nor to their admiration.

They hoped that Aunt Hegarty and the nieces would remain on board the pirate ship while they took the *Happy-Go-Gay* in tow, but courteously Aunt Hegarty declined their offer.

All they needed, she said, was an axe, and perhaps a pair of strong shoulders to do some chopping and start them off with a good pile of fuel.

Benjamin, Charleyboy and James promptly set to work, and

by nightfall the hold was stacked with enough quartered coconuts to see them home.

Their store cupboards had been replenished and their water casks filled. In return Sophie gave Gustus a lesson in making porridge.

Annie wished either to stay with the boys, or to have Charleyboy and Gustus on board the *Happy-Go-Gay* with her, as before.

They refused to do either, and Annie, unusually meek for her, agreed to put up with it.

'It isn't for long,' Sophie said as they parted from the boys at the top of the brigantine's ladder. 'Soon you will be taking them back with you to the orphanage.'

'I'd rather go to live with Aunt Hegarty,' said Annie abruptly.

'We don't want to live without Annie! Only for holidays!' said Charleyboy and Gustus, putting their fists in their eyes.

'Then you had all better come and live with me,' said Aunt Hegarty calmly. 'I shall have to send Bella a telegram and write to Matron about it. I shall have a great deal to teach you, Annie.'

'Yes, Aunt Hegarty!' said Annie meekly.

'All aboard?' said Henry in the jollyboat. He rowed them back to the *Happy-Go-Gay* where the goat and Captain Bligh behaved like castaways who had given up all hope of rescue.

The pirate ship waited until the *Happy-Go-Gay* was once more under way and steaming happily towards port, her fuel assured, her crew well fed and confident.

Then, like a large benevolent sheepdog she spread her sails and shepherded them homewards, keeping well apart yet close enough at hand in case of danger.

The sun shone, and Sophie spread her washing on the deck. Lucy's engines purred with much the same contentment as Captain Bligh, who was sitting on Annie's lap as she mended a rent in Sophie's dress. Rose wrote up their travels in the ship's log and Harriet peeled apples for a tart. Aunt Hegarty stood at the wheel watching for landfall, her heart full of deep gratitude that she was bringing her dear nieces (and several nephews as well) safely back to port. Emma milked the goat.

Another night and a day and the blue south seas turned to cooler northern ones, already the night stars were paling and the waves ran milky grey.

Home called them all now, and the stout little ferryboat nosed her way northward with a richer band of rust about her prow and on her paddles, and the unwritten legend of her adventures fast in her hold.

The paddles would not stop churning now, nor the engines toiling, nor Lucy stoking, nor Sophie cooking, nor Rose writing their adventures, nor Annie improving herself, nor Harriet caring for their comfort, nor Emma caring for her animals, nor Aunt Hegarty standing at the wheel, nor the brothers in the ship behind them keeping careful watch and guard over their sisters until the *Happy-Go-Gay* was home.

Some Other Puffins you Might Enjoy

Bedknob and Broomstick *Mary Norton*

Miss Price lived in a neat little house, and she visited the sick and taught the piano. In all the village there was none so ladylike as Miss Price, but Carey, Charles and Paul happened to know how she hurt her ankle – she'd fallen off a broomstick!

So, as the price of their silence, Miss Price cast a spell on a knob of Paul's bed: he had only to twist it a little and wish, and it would take them wherever they wanted to go anywhere in the world, or even into the past. No spell could have been more exciting, or had more unexpected results.

By the author of *The Borrowers*, for readers of eight and over.

Magic by the Lake *Edward Eager*

'Have you noticed the name on the cottage?' asked Katharine. She and the rest of her family had just arrived at their holiday cottage.

'Magic by the Lake,' said Martha. 'Doesn't it sound lovely? Don't you wish it were true?'

Then Mark's turtle stuck its head out of its shell. 'Now you've done it,' it said. 'You couldn't be sensible, could you, and order magic by the pound, for instance, or by the day? Or by threes, the good old-fashioned way? You had to be greedy and order magic by the lake, and of course now you've got a whole lakeful of it!'

Readers of *Half Magic* will already know Mr Eager's particular blend of enchantment, with its mixture of humour, wild adventure, and everyday happenings.

Saturday and the Irish Aunt *Jenifer Wayne*

Jessica, Nonnie and Ben had never met their grandfather while he was alive, and certainly didn't expect his will to be interesting – but they were wrong, for he had left each of them fifty pounds, *to spend exactly as they liked.*

Fifty pounds each! It was odd that in spite of their excitement they could think of so few practical ways of spending it that were neither too big nor too small. Jessica was bursting with schemes, like starting a pottery or building a theatre, and Ben was torn between ideas of modernizing his bedroom, motorbikes, and buying a cow. And Nonnie? She was in the worst dilemma of all, she had to choose between the lovely pony she longed to buy and saving grandfather's poor old mare in Ireland.

And then, as if the excitement wasn't already at boiling point, their Irish Aunt arrived.

Catweazle *Richard Carpenter*

Catweazle was a magician who lived in the 11th century, and usually his spells never worked. But one day was different, and he flew through Time instead of Space, and ended up on a place called Hexwood Farm nine centuries later, where of course he thought everything he saw – motor cars, telephones, electric light ('Eleck-trickery') – all happened by magic.

How Catweazle is befriended by the farmer's son, Carrot, and how he finds his feet in the 20th century, while hiding from the world in a water tower, makes a riotously funny story, as anyone who has seen the television serial will know.

For readers of eight and over.

My Friend Mr Leakey *J. B. S. Haldane*

Mr Leakey was the only magician who could bring a sock to life, or bewitch a tie-pin and a diary so that he could never lose them. He wanted to run over to Java after lunch, and was going to use a touch of invisibility in the morning to cure a dog that was always biting people.

If you want to know more about Mr Leakey and his household jinn and the octopus who served his meals and the dragon (wearing asbestos boots) who grilled the fish, you must read this book to find out.

For readers of eight and over.

Green smoke *Rosemary Manning*

R. Dragon was 1,500 years old, and he had a great partiality for almond buns. He was a dragon with impeccable manners, who was far too polite to eat people, and avoided meeting them because he did not like frightening them. He could also tell stories, and Sue heard about the Cornish giants and fairies, and of King Arthur whom he had known very well. He taught Sue songs and took her to tea with a mermaid, who told her about the country under the sea.

Altogether a charming 'someone' to discover, as every boy and girl from six to nine will find out for themselves.

If you have enjoyed this book and would like to know, about others which we publish, why not join the Puffin Club? You will receive the club magazine, *Puffin Post* four times a year and a smart badge and membership book. You will also be able to enter all the competitions. Write for an application form to:

The Puffin Club Secretary
Penguin Books Limited
Bath Road
Harmondsworth
Middlesex